PRESTON'S
HAUNTED
HERITAGE

PRESTON'S HAUNTED HERITAGE

By JASON KARL
& ADELE YEOMANS

First published in 2007
by Palatine Books,
Carnegie House,
Chatsworth Road
Lancaster LA1 4SL
www.palatinebooks.com

Researcher Sian Rayner

British Library Cataloguing-in-Publication data
A catalogue record for this book is available from the British Library

ISBN 10: 1-874181-41-1
ISBN 13: 978-1-874181-41-5

Designed and typeset by Carnegie Book Production
Drawings by Ivan Frontani

www.carnegiebookproduction.com
Printed and bound in the UK by Alden Press

INTRODUCTION

When I first came to Preston with the Discovery Channel in 1996, I had no idea that I would end up living here, or that I would end up mixing not only with its sentient residents, but also with its ethereal community ...

Genuine contemporary ghost stories are few and far between, but as you will see in Prestons Haunted Heritage, our city and the surrounding area boast a plethora of spectres just waiting to be discovered by the brave – or should they be called foolhardy!

It was during my first week in Preston that I was to come face to face with a very well known local ghost, a meeting that was definitely not strictly within the realm of the living. Samlesbury Hall's infamous White Lady is one the North West's most famous and well attested ghosts, with sightings of the phantom dating back decades, so I was keen during my research for this book to re-visit her old haunt, this time in the new millennium. It was a rewarding, if unsettling, experience and the White Lady didn't disappoint, as you can read in chapter three.

In 2005 I was invited to spend an afternoon at an historic manor house near Poulton le Fylde in the company of Mrs Adele Yeomans, who had invited me to bring a medium to investigate the ghostly goings on in her ancient home, Mains Hall. That afternoon was the beginning of a supernatural journey in which Adele and I decided to explore as many ancient haunts as possible and to create a spine tingling collection of books filled with true accounts that would both inspire the reader to find out more, and show them how to unlock the door to an eerie otherworld that lies unseen, yet within the grasp of us all.

When we began we hardly expected that we would find such a diverse range of hauntings, which include a 'toast ghost' in a funeral home, a ghost caught on film at an old inn in Kirkham, a haunted underground Mexican restaurant, a smelly ghost in a fancy dress agency and even a slip in time itself.

Sprawling halls, ancient manor houses, theatres and haunted homes; we have explored them all during our probing exploration of the supernatural side of Preston. As you go about your daily life in the urban sprawl of the city, take a moment to peak into the shadowy corners and cobbled alleyways, for it is here that traces of a long forgotten past still linger. As the seen meets the unseen in a city where not all is what it seems, take a walk on the other side as we take you on a terrifying tour in *Preston's Haunted Heritage*.

Happy hauntings!

Jason Karl
Halloween 2007
www.jasondexterkarl.com

ACKNOWLEDGEMENTS

We would like to thank: Anna, Alistair and Lucy at Carnegie Publishing for believing in this project and bringing it to fruition, and for allowing us to pursue our ghostly pursuits around Preston. The psychic mediums on this project: Veronica Charles, Angela Borrows, Sybil Lucas-Brewer. The researcher on this project, Sian Rayner. Owners, curators, innkeepers and custodians of the locations featured in the book, and in particular: Knicki Jones at DB Mex; Sharon Jones and Julie at Samlesbury Hall; Cassie and John at the Wheatsheaf Inn; Eileen Flanagan and Christine Daniels at Hoghton Tower; Maggie Murray for her account of the ghost at the Warren Funeral Home; Nicola White at Haighton Manor; Wendy Simpson, Carla Schmitz, Paul Howse and Simon Castle for their accounts of experiences at Eddington House; Maggie Murray of Cabaret Fancy Dress; David Adams Wilson of the Old Hob Inn; Alec Price for supplying information on Park Hall; Lisa Gillibrand, Jane Fletcher, Andrea Morris, Michelle Allsopp and Marilyn Deverill of Worden Hall; Pam Mobbs and Dave Eyre of the Hand and Dagger; Sandra Valentine and Collette of the Bell and Bottle; Cheryl Holmes, Niki Park and George at the Wellington Inn; David Summerville for his information on Alston Hall; Jackie Hargreaves of Preston Town Hall; Alex Tagg and Nick Tomlinson of the Playhouse Theatre; Pete Bony of the Paranormal Activity Research Team; and all other informers.

CHAPTER ONE

LIVING WITH THE DEAD

THE ARCHWAYS, PEDDERS LANE, PRESTON CITY

At the centre of Ashton Park on the outskirts of the city of Preston stands the once stately pile known as Ashton House. It is now in use as a childcare centre and as far as I know has no ghostly inhabitants, but its former stables just across the road are a different matter ...

Known as 'The Archways', the one-time stable yard and outbuildings are now a luxury suburban development of modern housing and my informant, who lives there, told me of the strange encounters she has experienced in her home.

"The first occurrence happened on the night I moved into the house. It was the middle of winter in December 2003 and the night was bitterly cold and dark. My brother was staying with me as he had helped me move in and as we had spent a long day moving furniture we decided to have an early night. It was the middle of the night when I was awoken by the sound of the bedroom door opening and soft footsteps, like bare feet, walk up to the edge of my bed and around to the other side. At this point my heart was pounding and I kept my eyes tightly shut, willing whatever it was to go away. But as I lay there in fear I felt a weight sit down on the bed and I rolled towards the dip in the mattress. By now I was in a state of panic; the experience seemed to continue for some time but in reality was probably only a matter of seconds before everything returned to normal. I opened my eyes and turned on the light to find nothing in the room. I quickly went to see if my brother had heard the footsteps but he was deeply asleep."

My other experience in this house happened in the summer of 2004 when I was in bed again! On this occasion I was awoken by the feeling of two hands around my ankle which were pulling me off the bed and I had the most peculiar scary feeling. At first I thought I must be dreaming but then when my arms were also pulled, though in another direction, I realised that the ghost was back. I was determined to open my eyes and as I looked around in the darkness I was shoved with force to the top of the bed – so hard that I actually bumped my head on the wall. I grabbed the light switch and slept with the room illuminated the rest of the night!"

Having had experiences with spirits all over the world, the lady who lives in this particular haunted home has opted to continue living with her ghostly incumbent, treating it not as a curiosity but rather as a simple matter of fact.

Sykes Lumb Farm, Near Preston

The ghost of old Dame Sykes, whose wizened form is seen still lurking around Sykes Lumb Farm, which was once their home, is probably one of Lancashire's oldest recorded sightings, dating back to the Wars of the Roses. This bitter civil war, pitched between the House of Lancaster and the House of York between 1455 and 1487, brought much unrest to the area, being not far from the borders of the two counties. The story goes that thrifty old man Sykes and his wife had grown very wealthy prior to the outbreak of the war, and, fearing that troops or marauders may invade and loot their property, they hid the bulk of their wealth in earthenware jars and buried them beneath the huge roots of an old apple tree in the orchard.

At this time, the childless couple had no-one to inherit the farm. Old farmer Sykes died very soon after the close of the war and his wife, Dame Sykes, died so suddenly after him, legend has it, that she did not have time to divulge the whereabouts of their booty. However, one could speculate that, as the couple were well known for being so miserly anyway, they would not wish anyone to find their well hidden 'treasure'. Close relatives of the couple, on hearing of their untimely demise, came searching for the money, but found nothing. As the years passed, many tenants came and went and none, despite their searches, could find the location of the money jars. Locals shunned the place at night, as it was soon believed to be haunted by the ghost of the old lady as she continued to wander aimlessly around what was once her property. Occasionally others saw her lurking in what had been the old barn. Locals speculated that she was guarding her treasure.

Year passed and the legend continued. The terrifying spectre continued to appear to any who were brave enough to venture into Dame Sykes' area of the Lumb. Eventually one dark night, a tenant (a gentleman who was fond of his ale) was staggering homewards towards the farm when he came upon the old lady's ghost as she continued about her nightly visitations. Fuelled perhaps with 'Dutch courage', he approached the haggard old form and watched silently as she glided ahead of him, pointing with her crooked old stick. Feeling that she wished him to follow, he dutifully did, and she slowly led him towards the dead stump of an old apple tree. Upon reaching the stump, she shook her stick vigorously at it and then she disappeared in front of his eyes. With that, he made a hasty retreat back to the warmth and comfort of the farm.

A few hours later, possibly when the drink had worn off, he still recalled the hideous old hag he had seen and remembered the place she had brought him to. Quickly, he roused the entire household and spades and forks were quickly found. The party dug for hours and, so legend tells, the old lady herself hovered nearby to watch their progress. All the time she hovered, her brow was wrinkled and her lips down turned in a disapproving scowl. Eventually the money jars were indeed found and as the last jar was brought to the surface, worried diggers looked to the old hag. To their astonishment, her scowl turned into a thin smile and at that moment she simply faded away and was apparently never seen again.

Although the family and the farm are no longer intact, a cottage now stands in the grounds of the former Sykes Lumb Farm. One can only assume old Dame Sykes is truly laid to rest now the money has been found ... unless you know otherwise?

HOLLAND FLATS, WALTON-LE-DALE

In May 2001 I received a long letter from the owner of a 100-year-old converted farmhouse and barn which now stands on a main road, but which at one time would have been quite rural. In the interests of privacy I have changed the names of the people involved, and for the purpose of relating their tale I shall call them Pat and John.

The disturbances which were to become the cause of intense fear over a number of months began early one sunny morning in May 1999. Pat was washing the breakfast dishes in the kitchen and daydreaming whilst looking out of the window when suddenly the peace was shattered by a loud, blood-curdling scream which emitted from within the room behind her. She span around terrified, only to find the room deserted and, rooted to the spot with fear and confusion, she looked into the dining room to find some possible explanation. It was then that she first felt the presence watching her. "It was the same kind of feeling when you know someone is looking at you at a party, but it was much, much more intense. It was then that my mind shifted to ghosts and the possibility that the house might be haunted. If only I had known what was to come, I might have packed up and left right then."

Later when John returned home from work Pat explained what had happened and he reassured her, telling her it must have come from a neighbouring house or been some kind of sound displacement from outside. However, that night at 2.30 a.m., they were awoken by the sound of someone running along the upstairs corridor towards their bedroom. Assuming it was one of their four children Pat got up to see what was the matter, but when she opened the door the corridor was deserted. She went in to check on her children and found one of them wide awake and in a state of shock. "The duvet was shaking, Mummy!", she said. Pat tucked her back in and returned to her bedroom, her mind racing with unanswered questions and creeping fear.

Over the proceeding days the phenomenon seemed to intensify, it was as if something evil had entered their lives and was tightening its grip. The next notable occurrence happened a couple of nights later when the entire household was awoken to the thunderous sound of loud banging coming from the dining room downstairs. The sound stopped abruptly as John set foot off the staircase and began to make his way towards the room from where the sounds seemed to emanate. Not surprisingly, when he opened the door there was nothing in the room which could explain the sounds. The very next day the ghost was back, this time it was heard by Pat sneezing on the staircase, and later the front door slammed in her face as she approached it, even though it was a still day with no breeze. By now the family were convinced they were being visited by forces from beyond the grave and as the occurrences grew more intense, so did their determination to fight them. It was a couple of days afterwards when, during the early evening, Pat and John were watching television in the lounge. John reached over to give Pat an affectionate kiss on the cheek when suddenly, as if in annoyance, a heavy glass candle holder flew off the stereo and right across the room. John picked it up and replaced it in defiance, but the second he had moved away it flew off again, at which point the defeated couple retired to bed, leaving the lounge to the ghosts for the night.

Footsteps, cold unexplainable draughts, interference with a vacuum cleaner and unexplainable scents all added to the catalogue of ghostly events over the following weeks, until late one night in April when the first apparition manifested itself in the kitchen. "It was an old man with a pale face and dark, sunken eyes", described John. "He looked at me before turning and walking through the dining room and out of the front door, which was closed at the time". Although Pat was present at the time of the sighting she witnessed nothing, but one of her daughters was soon to be visited by the strange man in her bedroom. "I woke up and there was a man in the room, he stooped over me and stared at me before kicking my bed and walking over to the window, where he disappeared", she said. I asked her to draw a picture of what she had seen; the resulting sketch shows a man wearing a neck ruff and tunic, with hollow staring eyes. After seeing this ghost she ran screaming into her parent's bedroom and spent the rest of the night under their close supervision.

The next evening the phantom man was back, although this time unseen, as the same daughter heard somebody riffling through her make-up and CDs. She ran out of the room and once again spent the night with her parents, but on this occasion she had not escaped. In the early hours of the following morning John was woken from his slumber by the feeling of a weight on his lower legs, and as his eyes were becoming accustomed to the dark he saw the figure of a middle-aged woman sitting on the bed, watching him. As he came to and rubbed his eyes the vision, and the weight, had gone.

With a wealth of evidence piling up for this case I decided to visit and take a psychic medium along with me to see if we could find out who was haunting this old farmhouse and why. Medium Angela Borrows and I arranged to visit the house in June 2001. After meeting the owners Angela decided to have a walk around the building to see if she could pick anything up before fully tuning in. As she ascended the staircase a scent of perfume became apparent to her, and on asking Pat about this was told that this was the same spot where the ghostly sneeze had been heard weeks earlier. As she continued up the stairs and along the corridor I followed in anticipation of what might occur. As we entered one of the bedrooms which Angela had been drawn to, a feeling of heavy oppression hit us both; it was as if the room had an unwelcoming atmosphere. Pat told us that the room we were standing in belonged to her daughter and was the site of the visitations of the man with sunken eyes. We decided to continue our investigation downstairs, but as we headed from the hall into the dining room we both stopped. It was very apparent to both of us that there was a very strong alcoholic smell which had not been there before we had gone upstairs. Both Angela and I likened the scent to that of beer, or hops. There was no explanation for it and the moment we acknowledged it, it dissipated, as is so often the way with evidence of a spectral nature.

After touring the home Angela felt that the spirits which had been disturbing the family were temporary hauntings and would not linger for long inside the house. I asked the family to contact me if anything further occurred to add to this ghostly dossier, but at the time of writing I have not heard from them again. I can therefore only assume that Angela was right and that the phantoms have moved on to haunt pastures new.

Moorbrook Lodge, Withnell, Chorley

Standing atop a hill in a shadowy glen at the end of a cobbled drive stands a house known as 'Moorbrook Lodge', originally built in 1775 and modified many times over the following centuries. The stone-built, 230-year-old house is the haunt of two wandering spirits who have been witnessed in a variety of ways, one on frequent occasions.

The first story concerns the ghost of a small boy who is blamed for interference on a music system in the dead of night. The current owner, who has lived there for over twenty years, told me of disturbed nights when the moon was high and the air deathly still. He had been woken on various occasions by the sudden and inexplicable function of the music system which is housed in the drawing room. He always ensured that the power button was switched off before retiring to bed, but despite that on many occasions a particular CD suddenly began to play at high volume apparently of its own accord, always the same CD and track number, which woke the entire household. If a power surge or forgetting to turn off the system could account for the sudden function, what can account for the track number always being the same? To play the track in question the 'forward' button would have needed to have been pressed to select it, otherwise the CD would of course begin at track 1. As I listened to the story it occurred to me that this meant the ghost had not only turned on the power and depressed the play button, but had also selected its desired track ...

The house is also haunted by the wraith of a woman whose identity is as yet unknown. I was told that whilst decorating the downstairs corridor in preparation for selling the property in early 2005 the owner's girlfriend was helping out with some painting, but had encountered a ghost and refused to work or sleep inside the building again. She described the sensation as that of someone rushing past her as she worked and that despite not labelling herself as a psychic, she had the strong impression that it was the spirit of a woman. Prior to interviewing the previous owner I took psychic medium Veronica Charles on a tour of the house, of which she had no prior knowledge. She immediately sensed that the fireplace area of the drawing room was connected with the wandering spirit of a woman – this fireplace is the other side of the corridor where the 'rushing lady' was encountered, so could this be the same spirit?

The atmosphere of the house is friendly and welcoming, but has that indisputable 'haunted' feeling that I have become attuned to over my lifetime dealing with ghosts and spirits. At the time of writing it had been for sale for over a year, but I am assured that is no longer the case. I wonder if the new owners have met their new ghostly house mates yet!

EMERSON ROAD, PRESTON CITY

This account of a disturbing haunting in Preston dates from the 1960s and was provided by an informant. I cannot do better than to quote verbatim from her letter:

"Judging from old photographs I must have been about 18 months old when we moved into Emerson Road. It was just an average house with three bedrooms and two reception rooms with a small kitchen at the back. It was never a happy house, always dark and gloomy, and the ten years I spent growing up there always seemed tainted by what happened.

I first recall something strange happening when I was eight years old, my father was reading me a bedtime story, my mother was out and we were alone in the house. We were disturbed by a loud knocking on my bedroom door, not a scratching, nor a tapping, but a loud 'answer the door' sort of knock. I looked at my father and he looked back at me, apprehension in his eyes, which unnerved me as he was usually such a strong man. He stood up and went over to the closed door and opened it, walking onto the landing and disappearing from view. Minutes later he returned and told me not to worry, that there was no-one there and everything was fine. He continued to read me the story and then I went to sleep.

Nothing further happened until nearly two years later when, after discussing ghosts with my mother and father over dinner one evening, I was reminded of the incident and asked my father if he recalled it. He told me that he did, and that the same thing had happened on numerous occasions with some regularity over a long period of time in the house, although not on my bedroom door, always on theirs.

Some time later I discovered that a favourite book of mine had disappeared. We searched high and low in the small house for this book but it was nowhere to be found, so in the end we gave up looking resigning ourselves to its loss. But that wasn't the end of the book, as you will see ...

The next encounter I recall happened on a very cold winter's night – it was so cold in fact that I can remember seeing ice patterns on the inside of my bedroom window. It was the early hours of the morning and I was unable to settle that night. The silence was suddenly broken by the faint sound of shuffling outside my bedroom door, at first very faint but gradually growing louder until I was sure there was something outside my door waiting to enter my bedroom. Unable to contain my fear any longer I let out a piercing scream which brought my father running into my room to calm me down. I told him what I had heard and he reassured me that I had imagined it. He checked the wardrobe and under my bed to show me that I was safe but as he turned to leave the room it began again. A definite limping or shuffling noise, so loud now that it was as if something was inside the room with us. My father collapsed, shaking his head in his hands, but moments later he was up on his feet, determined to face this invisible foe and stand steadfast against it. He searched the house again, finding nothing, but as he returned to my bedroom he became transfixed on the small fireplace in the corner, a fireplace we never used I might add. He explained later that he was compelled to approach it, and after doing so he stuck his head inside, looking up into the blackened chimney. There, covered in soot was the book which had disappeared weeks earlier, stuffed way up the chimney and wedged so that it would not fall out. How it got there is still a mystery, but it was soon confined to the dustbin and not mentioned again.

We moved out soon after that night, into rented accommodation until we could find a new home. My father died aged 74 and continued to talk of the haunting at Emerson Road right up to the day of his death. He always held the opinion that despite living in fear of our phantom house guest it was the living you should fear, not the dead!

I found out many years later that the previous occupant of the house had committed suicide there, hanging himself in the room I slept in. Perhaps it was he who had caused the shuffling sounds and knocking and who stuffed my book up the chimney – a sad lonely spirit who was unable to rest in peace."

PARKER STREET, ASHTON UPON RIBBLE

In February 1996 I was contacted by a local newspaper journalist who asked me if I would visit a house where a young couple had experienced strange activity which they believed was due to the presence of a ghost. Of course I was happy to take up the case and to investigate this haunted home and I took along psychic medium Sybil Lucas-Brewer.

It was a cold February day when we located the quiet Victorian terraced house and met the young couple who had just purchased the property as their first home together. It was their dream home when they had agreed to buy it but since moving in they had experienced a plethora of paranormal activity that totally petrified them, so much so that they even refused to use the toilet alone. I asked the owners (who wish to remain anonymous) what had been occurring in the house and they began regaling me with anecdotes of rattling cupboards, the strong smell of pipe smoke, a toilet flushing by itself at 3.00 a.m., and the feeling of a man brushing his hands through their hair. One said: "We sensed it as soon as we first moved in. There was something strange about the house. Every time I open the bedroom curtains I get a chill down my spine – it's got so bad that I won't even stay on my own in the house". We assured the couple that we would get to the bottom of the haunting if we could and with that the investigation began. Sybil was instantly drawn to the staircase – "we need to go up", she said. After climbing the staircase Sybil walked into the front bedroom. "Is this the window where you feel a chill?", she asked the owners, and it turned out that it was. Sybil sat on the edge of the bed and started to go into a trance state to try to contact the spirit so that I could speak to it and find out why it was haunting the house. After a few minutes I looked at Sybil – whose breathing had become shallow, which I knew was an indication that she was deep in trance – who said "hello, what is your name?" "William", came the abrupt reply from Sybil's mouth but in a deeper, gruff voice. Before I could speak again the spirit spoke through Sybil: "Where is Mable?" "Who is Mable?", I asked. By communicating with the spirit through Sybil I was able to ascertain that he was waiting for a kindly neighbour to deliver a meal to him, that she was called Mable and she always brought him a cooked dinner on a tray each evening. I asked the spirit if he knew that he had passed on from this life, at which point he became confused and asked for Mable again. After a couple of minutes it became apparent that he had suffered greatly towards the end of his life with bronchial problems which had meant he was unable to use the stairs and therefore his meals were brought to him. He had waited patiently at the window each evening to watch for Mable arriving but was confused as to why she no longer came. Through gentle persuasion I was able to ask him to pass on and to leave the home he had loved so much in life, and Sybil ensured that he went off to the next plane of existence and would haunt the couple no more.

After Sybil came out of trance and had rested for a short while we asked the owners if they had known about the previous occupier of the house. It all made sense when they told us that an old man had lived here alone and had died upstairs in the house from a bronchial condition.

The outcome of this investigation lends support to the theory that many spirits are unaware that they have died and that sometimes all that is needed is a medium and a sympathetic ear to help an unhappy spirit find peace.

EDDINGTON HOUSE, ASHTON UPON RIBBLE

A Victorian town house once named Eddington House is the scene of this next haunting tale, recorded by myself in a 'Ghost Diary' during the eight years I inhabited the house. As soon as I saw the building I had a feeling it was haunted. Despite its dilapidated appearance and terrible 1960s interior decor there was an atmosphere about it, and we moved in on Halloween, which I think paved the way for things to come ...

Built in 1880 the 125-year-old house has been altered and adapted many times and our intensive renovation programme was the last makeover this haunted home has undergone. We had only been in the house for a matter of hours before strange things started to happen. I decided to take some photographs of the rooms before we commenced work and recall at the time thinking to myself 'if there is anything haunting this house please come out on the photographs'. Expecting nothing to appear I was amazed when days later I discovered white streaks of light on several of the developed prints, for which there was no explanation, and they remain a mystery to this day.

Days later I wrote in the Ghost Diary:

"We hadn't actually moved in yet because there was a lot of structural work which needed doing beforehand such as removing built-in wardrobes and fixtures and re-opening up the four fireplaces. It was during the unblocking of the last upstairs fireplace that I first felt something unusual. I was alone in the house for the first time, which didn't bother me as it has a friendly welcoming atmosphere, and I was busy removing bricks and rubble from the fireplace in what is to be the second bedroom when I became mentally aware that I was being observed. I was not surprised by the feeling as I have experienced lots of strange things in my life which I have put down to ghosts, and to tell the truth I was excited at the feeling that we might have a ghost in our new house. The feeling subsided after a short while and I thought little more about it."

That initial experience took place during the day on a cold early November afternoon; the next event, however, happened during the night several days later and was witnessed by my partner, Simon.

Simon remembers:

"I awoke for no apparent reason and was instantly rigid with fear; a shiver went down my spine which sounds very dramatic but is actually what happened. Although I could see nothing (it was dark anyway) I am absolutely convinced that someone was standing on the threshold of the room, just around the door which was open to my right. At the time I could feel that it wanted to come into the room – I am just glad it didn't!"

In late January 1999 we received a gift of an armchair for the new upstairs study which was almost complete. In the meantime the chair was to be kept in the blue drawing room downstairs. It arrived on Saturday 30th via my parents who had come up to stay for the weekend,

and it was in the kitchen that evening that the conversation between my mother and me turned to ghosts...

"I was telling Mum what had happened in the house and showed her the four strange photographs. One of the comments I made was that although I had witnessed countless ghostly events in my life I had never seen anything move, and that I would very much like to. It was just a comment and I forgot about it as soon as I had said it, but it appears from what happened a few days later that the ghosts did not forget."

The following Tuesday I was finishing painting the upstairs study and came down for lunch. I went into the blue drawing room and noticed immediately that the small gold armchair which had been next to the left hand wall had moved six feet and was now next to the window, positioned as if someone sitting on it could look out into the front garden! There seemed to be no reasonable explanation for the movement. However, the house was home to two young boisterous cats, could they have moved the chair in any way? I don't think this could be the case as the force required to move it would be far greater than that of two young cats. Add to this the fact that the chair had swivelled to face a different direction as well as moving across the room and it becomes even more of an enigma.

It is interesting to note that the date on which the chair moved may have some supernatural significance. The 2 February is the Pagan festival of Imbolc, a time which has links with Wicca, Paganism and magic. Perhaps this had something to do with the phenomenon of the moving chair?

I decided to invite a professional sensitive into the house and thus spiritualist medium Joyce Thorne found herself spending a day at Eddington House, and it was during this visit that she sensed the presence of several different wraiths residing in the building.

Joyce said: "I first sensed very strongly a nineteenth-century couple, the man wearing a top hat, a grey cravat with a white pearl pin, shiny boots, a high collar shirt, and a flower in his button hole. The lady was small and round-faced, she was wearing a bonnet and crinoline dress. I felt that they were a very loving couple who had lived in the building in the past; they enjoyed the company of others and regularly invited people into their home. They seemed to be very happy that the new owners were returning the house to its former glory. They loved the house dearly and were very happy here, which is why they still remain and are loath to leave. They are accompanied by a small King Charles spaniel dog, light brown and white in colour which has a small bell on its collar. The dog is a much-loved pet.

I also sensed the presence of a different spirit from another era. This spirit is a Victorian gentleman sporting a monocle and van Dyke beard with a distinctly Dickensian appearance, sharp features and bright blue eyes. He seemed to have a scientific mind and an enquiring nature. Although his appearance would lead you to believe he is stoical and logical, it actually belies his true personality which is deeply sensitive. He told me that he was 'not easily bamboozled' in life and saw the truth of all situations that he became involved with. Generally the house has an atmosphere of liveliness and fun, perhaps because of the nineteenth-century ghosts, and this atmosphere eases between serene, mellow, happy times to lively and excited times – both very good vibrational genius loci. The house also told me that Christmas time has been very important in its past because of its 'good cheer'. Lastly, a third faint memory came through involving a small child, a girl called Marietta – somebody was saying 'naughty Marietta', and I felt that she was a mischievous child who died fairly young, probably in her early teens. Her memory is strong because she had a wonderful bright spirit."

Following Joyce's visit two strange twists in this tale occurred. Firstly, on hearing the medium's account of the ghosts in the house Simon suddenly remembered that after being in the house for a couple of weeks a thought had come into his mind that a young girl had died in the house, aged around 15 years. At the time this seemed no more than a passing thought, especially as Simon is not usually psychic, but what is strange is that no-one other than him knew about this thought as he had not mentioned it to anyone. How then did it fit in with what the medium had said?

The next manifestation happened on Monday 8 March 1999 at 11.30 a.m. It was witnessed by me and I was alone in the house once again, except for the cats. I recorded it in the diary:

"I went downstairs to get a drink from the kitchen and as I walked through the red drawing room I passed through a strong, sweet scent which stopped me in my tracks and for which there was no apparent reason. It was like sweet flowers, perhaps sweet peas or peonies. We didn't have any flowers anywhere in the house at the time, so I put it down to the ghosts and walked into the kitchen. After a few steps I couldn't smell it at all; it was like walking out of a perfume shop and within a matter of feet the smell was completely unnoticeable. I walked back to the spot where the scent had been pungent and it was still there, but much milder and within two or three seconds it was gone completely. I walked around the room but there was no scent to be found. I still cannot explain what it could have been to this day".

The following month I was alone in the house, working in the study upstairs, when "I suddenly heard a clattering from the kitchen downstairs of crockery being moved around or knocked over. My instant reaction was that it was one of the cats up on the work surface looking for any scraps of food on the plates to be washed up, so I went downstairs to tell them off and to move the plates out of reach. But when I got to the kitchen they were no where to be seen. I came back upstairs and found one of them asleep in the master bedroom and the other asleep under the study armchair, so it couldn't have been either of them."

Later the same month one of the cats had a change of behaviour:

"Gobbolino is a very sensitive cat, he doesn't like strangers and is always the first to run and hide rather than stand up for himself, he has always been that way and we are used to his behaviour pattern, but then he started doing something slightly out of character, always at the bottom of the staircase. He began to make a noise we had never heard before, a sort of 'crying', and he always made it in the same spot, as if he was trying to tell us something was there, or something is 'frightening' or 'challenging' him. He also appeared to 'watch' things moving around the red drawing room that we were unable to see."

Another diary entry on Tuesday 15 June 1999 states:

"I was in the study with my back turned to the door looking at some papers when I saw in my peripheral vision a shadow move across the wall to my left. I paid no attention to it as this exact occurrence takes place every time someone enters that room because of the positioning of the lights. However, after a couple of seconds I turned round expecting to see who had entered and there was nobody there. A couple of hours later while in the master bedroom looking through some clothes in a box, once again with my back to the door of the room, I felt someone enter the room behind me. It didn't strike me as ghostly until I turned round and again there was nobody there."

June proved to be a busy month for Eddington House's ghostly residents as a couple of weeks later my diary says:

"I was washing my face at the bathroom sink and saw out of the corner of my right eye a movement of something black near the floor and going underneath the bath, which at the time had no side panel on it. I paid little attention as I simply assumed it was our cat Sootica, who is black and who often plays around the bath area. It was only after a couple of seconds that I realised that no cat could fit under the centre of the bath itself as there is only a few inches to squeeze through and so I looked around the room and beneath the bath only to find that there was nothing there. I immediately made a search of the house and found Sootica in a deep sleep in the master bedroom and our other cat was not in the house."

That was only the first appearance of the ghost cat, for he was to return a few days later.

"It was late afternoon and as I turned into the bathroom I clearly saw a black cat standing on the green carpet just inside the study, by the open door. The ghost faded in a couple of seconds but I recognised it at the time as Casper, our last cat who sadly was killed on a road near our last house."

On Monday 12 July 1999 one of our friendly spirits lent Simon a helping hand:

"I have to be at work early in the morning and on this particular occasion I needed to find a business card which I had left lying around somewhere the previous evening. I thought I had left it in the red drawing room on the sideboard amongst some other papers, but on inspection I could not find it. I pulled out my file case from beneath the stack of documents and placed it on the arm of the sofa; it is a black leather case and there was nothing on top of it to my knowledge. After searching thoroughly and becoming increasingly agitated I decided to look in the study upstairs. The card was nowhere to be seen and so I gave up and went back to the red drawing room to pick up my jacket. As I entered the room I saw in front of me the white business card lying in the exact centre of my black leather case file! It had not been there before, I cannot possibly have overlooked it. It is an understatement to say I was astonished, but grateful!"

Later the same day I was to witness some unusual behaviour by our black cat Sootica.

"I was tidying the upstairs rooms when I heard her meowing from downstairs; she often does this to see where I am, and in response I called out to her. She bounded up the staircase in her usual way, but then stopped dead at the doorway to the master bedroom. She stood there staring into the room, at what appeared to me to be absolutely nothing. Because of her unusual reaction I ceased what I was doing and observed her. She reluctantly entered the room as if concentrating hard on some unseen thing that she could see and I could not. Her movements within the room were not characteristic of her normal behaviour and she seemed distinctly nervous and hesitant. Whatever she could see what obviously floating above her and must have been 'all-encompassing' within the room rather than 'moving' because of the way she was observing 'it'. I picked her up to comfort her and to observe her reaction and I put her on the bed. She continued to act in the same way and shortly made her way out of the room. When out of the room she looked back in the room as if to check whether it was still 'occupied', which apparently it was, so she went swiftly downstairs and outside."

On Saturday 31 July 1999 the helpful ghost returned, this time helping me.

"I got up early to do some paperwork in the study. Just before 9.00 a.m. Gobbolino came into the room and jumped onto my lap, noticing my silver steel pen on the desk in front of me – he seems to have a penchant for pens! After staring at it for a few moments he reached over and grabbed it before jumping off my lap and playing with it on the carpet next to me. A couple of minutes later I needed it but he had gone and so had the pen! I went and found him downstairs and had a root round for the pen, but it was nowhere to be seen. I assumed he had knocked it under a chair and went back to the study. When I entered the room the pen was lying on the desk! There is no way a cat could have put it there. I don't know how it got there, all I know is that somehow it got back on top of the high desk while no cat or person was in the room."

Autumn seems to wake that which may otherwise be sleeping and at Eddington House this seemed to be the case one October night. I had been out for the evening with my friend Kerri, she often stays and is used to the building. Kerri told me the next morning:

"I went to sleep as usual in the second bedroom but woke up in the early hours for no apparent reason. As soon as I was awake I was aware that there was a man sitting in a chair in the right hand corner of the room, near the fireplace. I couldn't actually see anything as it was so dark but I know he was there … I could feel him in the room."

Exactly a year and a day after restoration work began Simon had his second frightening experience; it took place in the early hours of 31 October 1999 – Halloween. Simon recalls:

"I awoke in the early hours of the morning, I don't know what woke me up but lying there in the master bedroom trying to get back to sleep I distinctly heard the squeak of a floorboard either on the landing or on the step into the master bedroom. I am used to hearing this as the floorboards always make that sound as someone crosses them. It struck me as unusual at the time for some reason and so I got up and turned on the light in the stairwell – nothing there to account for the noise, no cats and no people. I then went into the second bedroom and found Sootica curled up fast asleep on the bed. At this point I became nervous as I realised she had been asleep for a while and the other cat was shut downstairs. I went back to bed considerably scared and even thought about waking Jason as I did not want to meet whatever had been moving around outside the bedroom door. I know all old houses creak and groan from time to time but this sound was the same as when someone crosses this particular area of the house, and this house, despite being old, is a quiet and settled one – well most of the time!"

Three months passed quietly before the next encounter, which occurred on a Sunday lunchtime in February 2000 and was experienced by a friend – Carla Schmitz – who was staying with us. She said:

"While getting dressed in the second bedroom I heard what I thought was either Jason or Simon coming upstairs. I heard three treads on the bare wooden staircase and then nothing. I went out and looked down the stairs but there was no-one there. I passed it off by summising that someone had started to come upstairs and then gone back down again. A couple of minutes later I went downstairs to ask who it was, and was surprised and a little afraid to hear that neither Jason or Simon had left the red drawing room, and that neither of them had heard any sounds. The footfalls were quite distinct and at the time did not seem unusual."

Carla stayed with us again on the night of Monday 6 March 2000 when she awoke to see a bright flash of yellow and white light on the wall, and she described seeing a friendly looking young girl's face staring out at her. It remained for only a couple of seconds before it was gone.

Could this be the ghost of Marietta, the 'bright young spirit' described by medium Joyce Thorne and sensed falling down the stairs by Simon? Several patterns were now beginning to emerge with the haunting of Eddington House.

At the beginning of May, Carla required a room to stay in for a while so we converted the blue drawing room into another bedroom and she moved in temporarily. On Tuesday 16th she met another of the esoteric residents.

"It was 11.00 a.m. and I was getting ready to go out, I had my CD player on and was dancing around by the front window. I turned around to face the wall opposite the window and I saw what I can only describe as the outline of a tall and fairly large man. I turned back to the window immediately to see if it could be a shadow or reflection of some kind but it wasn't. When I turned back towards the 'outline' it was still there. Rather than scaring me this sighting made me feel happy and I smiled; somehow the 'ghost' was exuding a sense of protection over me. I also had the name 'George' come into my head for some reason. A few seconds later it faded and was gone."

It was not long before Carla had her next encounter.

"Much later the same day, approximately 11.30 p.m., I got into bed to go to sleep and a strange feeling came over me. I sensed that a small female child was going to put her hands under the duvet and tickle my feet, so I quickly moved my feet away from the edge of the bed."

Another spectre made its presence known on Sunday 18th June, this time in the form of a motionless image of an old woman about five feet two inches in height standing in the middle of the red drawing room. I glimpsed her momentarily, but long enough to notice that she was wearing a garment which resembled a dressing gown and her hair was tied up in a short bun style. This was the first and only time anyone encountered the 'Dressing Gown Lady', as we affectionately labelled her.

The following Thursday night Wendy Simpson, another friend, was staying with us. She had spent the night many times before and had never experienced anything of a ghostly nature, but that was all about to change. Wendy said:

"I turned out the light and laid down to go to sleep in the bedroom on the right of the staircase as you ascend. I saw a brief flash of lights on the wall in front of me, so brief it is hard to say how many there were. This was at approximately 1.30 a.m. Later at about 3 a.m./4 a.m. I awoke and felt someone or something very gently squeeze my big toe, again very briefly. I sat up and looked around the room and there was nothing to explain what I had felt, so I laid back down and pulled my feet under the duvet as they had been protruding beforehand, and went back to sleep. Both incidents occurred on the same night within a few hours of each other but I did not feel threatened. It is difficult to ascertain whether the flashes were in front of me, or actually on the wall in hindsight."

At the time of her encounter Wendy, although aware that the house was 'haunted', was not aware of Carla's previous sighting of 'lights' in this room, or of the alleged haunting by the spirit girl Marietta. It was strange that Wendy should experience a touching on her toe – exactly what Carla felt was going to happen to her earlier in the year.

Simon was next to report a ghostly experience, which happened at 11.38 p.m. on a Monday night in July.

"I was lying in bed dozing and for some reason I opened my eyes and I saw in front of me, above the mirror on the chimney breast, a strange 'glow' which was moving in a random or sporadic fashion. The only thing I can compare the light to would be that caused by a lighted candle in a strong breeze, but there were no candles lit at the time, and no light source to account for what I was seeing. At the time it struck me that it may be my eyes playing tricks on me so I looked intently at another area of the room but could see nothing. When I looked back at the chimney breast the 'ghost glow' was still there. The sighting lasted approximately one minute and then promptly faded away. I then called Jason into the room to tell him what had happened."

Four months later on a cold Friday night in October 2000 Simon and I were watching a film in the red drawing room, which was in darkness apart from the light caused by the television screen.

"I got up off the sofa to change seats and as I stood up an extremely loud 'crack' noise was heard. We both heard it and it seemed to come from no one direction, rather the sound originated from the centre of the room itself. After turning the lights on and searching the room for a possible explanation, none could be found. However, the following morning I noticed in the mirror that part of my necklace had disappeared and was nowhere to be seen. I thoroughly searched the entire house, in particular the red drawing room where I had spent most of the previous night, but to no avail; the pendant (a bright turquoise cone) was not found. I then left the house for work. The Ghost Diary entry reads:

"I was really upset that I had lost the pendant as it had special sentimental feelings attached to it. I thought I must have lost it while I had been at the gym the day before. I telephoned to enquire if anyone had found and handed in the pendant, but it had not been reported. An hour or so later Simon rang me and told me that he had found the pendant lying exactly in the middle of the fire hearth in the red drawing room, pointing perfectly into the centre of the room. It was definitely not there when I searched the floor of that room, including the fire hearth, earlier that day."

Perhaps this 'placement' is connected with the unexplainable 'crack' noise which was experienced in the same room the night previous to this incident? It is also relevant to remember that the 'placement' of a business card which had been lost occurred in this room during July 1999 and a pen was 'placed' in the study during the same month.

In July 2001 we agreed that the house could be used as a location for the filming of a video presentation about the supernatural, largely filmed in the red drawing room and featuring myself and psychic medium Angela Borrows. After the crew left at 9.45 p.m., a sudden drop in temperature caused Angela and myself to exchange glances as we both felt the icy chill envelop the room and then moments later return to normal. There was no explanation for this radical ambient temperature fluctuation, but later that night, at around 3.30 a.m., Angela experienced something unseen blowing gently on her face six times as she tried to get to sleep on the couch in the red drawing room; there was no malevolent feeling associated with her encounter, merely playfulness.

After living in the house for some time it was becoming ever more apparent that we were sharing our home with several ghostly guests who were becoming more prevalent in their manifestations, as an encounter noted in my diary on 30 September 2001 indicates:

"I was taking some video footage of the blue drawing room and was surprised to find that when I played back the tape a strange globular ball of light whizzed through the frame and towards the door. Nothing was seen at the time and it was filmed during the day on a normal setting, not at night with an infrared camera when these anomalies are usually seen. The next day I planned to copy the tape to ensure its longevity but as I began it came off the spool and was destroyed beyond repair – almost as if the ghosts did not want me to have it!"

Almost a year later in August 2002 two mediums stayed with me and reported a feeling of unease in the house, particularly centring on the blue drawing room and the spare bedroom (formerly the study). Whilst staying overnight they both reported hearing scratching and tapping sounds which they could not account for, and also the 'swishing' of an unseen dress. Perhaps this was Marietta, or could it have been the Dressing Gown Lady?

Christmas was the time of our next recorded encounter, on Friday 27 December 2002. We found Simon's bank cash card, which had been securely in his wallet earlier in the day, placed in the middle of the floor in the master bedroom by some unseen hand. Sixteen quiet months followed and then in April 2004 Paul Howse, one-time President of The Ghost Research Foundation, was staying in the spare bedroom. He had heard that the house was haunted but had been given no information as to the nature of the spirits. He awoke at 6.00 a.m. and remembers hearing a distinct 'hello' in his ear, although he was alone in the room at the time!

The last encounter with the ghostly residents in this charming house occurred on 15 September 2005. I had been away for several days working and returned to the house during a heavy thunderstorm. I was glad when this journey was over and as I opened the front door I was surprised to see one of my cats, Pumpkin, coming down the staircase to greet me. Nothing strange in that you may think, but the odd thing is that the doors to all other rooms where firmly shut, keeping all the cats in their rightful place downstairs, so how had this cat found his way upstairs? He must have got in as Simon left this morning, I assumed, and thought no more about it. Later that evening Simon returned home and I mentioned that one of the cats had been upstairs all day, at which point Simon looked vexed. "But he couldn't have been upstairs, I saw him crouching beneath a tree as I left in the rain this morning. I definitely remember seeing him there as I felt sorry for him being stuck outside in the rain all day!" So this begs the question, how did Pumpkin get into an area of the house which is shut off by several closed doors? Perhaps one of

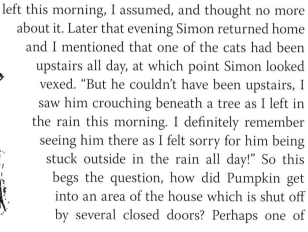

Eddington's friendly ghosts had felt sorry for him and opened the front door to let him shelter from the rain!

After eight years I left Eddington House and its ghostly residents behind, but I still have fond haunting memories of the Victorian Couple, the Monocle Man, Casper the black cat, the Dressing Gown Lady and Marietta, and I hope that the next incumbents of the house live in harmony with those that have gone before, and that the spirits remain in their home as the friendly ghosts of Eddington House.

CHAPEL LANE, HOGHTON

I received an invitation to visit a haunted terraced cottage on Chapel Lane in the village of Hoghton some years ago, after the family who lived there were experiencing various kinds of unexplained activity which they were becoming increasingly concerned about.

The owner, whom I shall call 'Jane', told me that they had lived in the house for over ten years and that the activity began when they first moved in 1986.

"I was decorating one summer evening and was on my own painting a wall on the landing when suddenly a thunderous noise like something very heavy being dragged along the floor broke the calm. It continued for a short while and then happened again a week later when a friend who was with me at the time heard it too."

After that initial incident a variety of strange occurrences were to follow over the next ten years. Jane continued:

"It kept taking our possessions which disappeared without trace and were then found months later in strange places. Some very important travel documents, a wrist watch and eighty pounds in cash all disappeared at different times. The documents never reappeared but we found the watch and the money in a box in my bedside cabinet!"

The family reported that the activity continued over time and they began to hear rattling door latches, footsteps and to experience a recurrent 'cold spot' in the lounge. Then one dark night Jane was to experience a truly frightening encounter in her son's bedroom, as she later reported to me:

"I decided to sleep in his room because he was complaining of hearing strange noises and I wanted to hear them for myself. As I was trying unsuccessfully to get off to sleep a creeping feeling of an icy chill went down the left hand side of my body, and I felt a sharp feeling as if a bony finger was prodding my leg and then my arm. I froze rigid with fear for what seemed like an age but was probably only a matter of thirty seconds or so, before the sensation subsided and the chill stopped. I raced out of the room and slept with my son and husband in our bedroom that night!"

Some nights later Jane's husband, who had never believed in anything supernatural, decided he would spend the night in their son's bedroom to prove that it was all in their minds. But he too experienced the icy chill and watched as the door opened of its own volition to reveal a hazy figure standing, and watching him, on the landing. It was the family's pet dogs who were next to encounter the ghost haunting the cottage. They would watch, spellbound, as some unseen 'thing' would move around the lounge and were unable to settle inside the home. Eventually one dog had to be re-homed as it had become so anxious and uncomfortable in the building.

By now the family were under no illusion that they were sharing their quaint country cottage with an unwelcome visitor whose activity seemed to be on the increase. Knocking on the front door and disturbing the family became a favourite trick of the chilly spook, but it was only Jane's husband who had actually seen it. Until one cold winter's evening, that is, as Jane recounts:

"I was making tea in the kitchen when out of the corner of my eye I caught a glimpse of the back of a beige-coloured coat which was walking past the kitchen door towards the staircase. I immediately put the tea tray down and ran into the hallway, but there was nothing to be seen, no coat and no figure. On recollection it had no head, which seems particularly odd to me!"

CHAPTER TWO

HOSPITABLY HAUNTED

Halfway House Inn, Clayton le Woods

On Preston Road in Clayton le Woods, just south of Bamber Bridge, lies the Halfway House pub. Here, three ghosts seem to have made themselves at home and in the 1990s were becoming more than a nuisance to the manager at the time and his staff. Two of the spirits seem 'friendly', polite even, as one says 'Excuse me' whenever he passes someone. The third phantom is considered not so friendly, and has in fact been described as a mischievous spirit, who has been nicknamed 'Sid'.

It all seemed to start when renovations were begun in 1999, although it may well be that there have been hauntings here for decades which have largely gone unreported. Staff member Paul Hayes said 'Sid' was most often seen or heard in the cellar. He turns lights on and off, which may be an almost childish prank to 'Sid' but certainly does not seem such a good idea to the staff, who refused to go down alone to change the barrels. He also emanates a certain malevolence at times, which makes people not wish to hang around in the vicinity for too long.

Another entity is heard stomping up the stairs which lead to the staff quarters, and there are rattling noises like doors being opened and then closed. A third presence likes to sit in the bay window of the pub, before melting into the background – literally!

Apparently the pub dates back to the 1700s where it began life as a coaching house and where frequent travellers stopped off seeking shelter, food and accommodation for the night. Little is known about the origins of these phantoms or who they are to this day, although their high jinx continues.

THE SPINDLEMAKERS ARMS, PRESTON CITY

Although now derelict, this old pub has had some unusual poltergeist activity. In the winter of 1991, just a few months before the pub was closed for good, recently appointed landlord and landlady Philip and Laura Boyes began reporting extremely strange events. A mysterious mist, intense freezing cold spots, footsteps, rappings, knockings, furniture being moved around at night and a loud coughing have all added to the legend of the Spindlemakers' haunting. Not only were the incumbents subjected to these random sounds and unnatural feelings, but personal items soon began to go missing, only to reappear days later and in what the couple describe as 'odd places'. The couple, who had two young children at the time, were afraid that these occurrences would frighten their children and became so worried that they called in a local psychic James Byrne in an attempt to get rid of this unwelcome addition to the family.

The Boyes had been forewarned about the ghosts of the Spindlemakers Arms but believed the legend to be nothing more than lighthearted banter. But they soon realised that almost everyone who came into the pub had had an encounter of some kind. Cleaning lady Marion Flannery, who was working there at the time, became so frightened after having seen 'something' whilst going about her business in the pub that she refused to work alone there. Most baffling of all was the very personal items, including jewellery, keys and even items of clothing from their wardrobe, which seemed to disappear then reappear elsewhere.

Months later, a local newspaper article reported the stories and within a short period of time the place was listed in the pub guides as 'closed/derelict'. As the old place now stands silently abandoned it is tempting to speculate that it is the ghosts of the Spindlemakers that have eventually frightened everyone away.

The Hand & Dagger, Treales, Kirkham

This seems to be quite a recent haunting and it could well be that there is more still to be discovered about the ghost who frequents this seventeenth-century watering hole. Landlord Dave Eyre and his partner Pam Mobbs have found their recent role as custodians here a little disconcerting, to say the least.

'Fred', as he has been affectionately named, seems to manifest his presence in several ways. Beer mats and menu cards get moved around during the night and even the tables and chairs have been found in different positions from those they had been left in the night before. Pam has said she can often hear male voices in the restaurant which is situated upstairs, even when there is no-one in there.

Locals seem familiar with 'Fred' and have warned the couple about his previous escapades. Whilst Pam says she is not frightened – yet – she would still very much like to get to the root of who this phantom 'beer mat juggling' ghost really is.

The Bell & Bottle, Kirkham

The Kirkham Bypass, as the A583 from Blackpool to Preston is known, has several old public houses, but one in particular has a reputation for at least two hauntings. The Bell and Bottle looks like a fairly modern building but it actually dates back at least 150 years, if not more. Historical details are sketchy but the people who have had the pleasure of residing there are convinced that there are more than just spirits of the alcoholic variety in this pub.

The stairs to the pub and an upstairs corridor appear to be haunted by a phantom of unknown origin. The first recorded account of a haunting comes from the owners of the inn during the late 1960s. Kathleen Eyre, writing in 1974 in *Lancashire Ghosts*, observes that previous owners had reported that "their dogs were nervous of going up the 'haunted' stairs". And the ghost of a young lad has also been witnessed by a group of people who could scarcely believe their eyes as his filmy shape appeared in what is now the restaurant of the building. This young man is thought to be a stable boy who, local legend tells

us, was kicked to death by his horse in this area where formerly the stables were housed.

At the time of writing, current landlady Collette says she is often 'spooked' whilst staying in the pub on her own after hours. She hears things on the stairs, sounds like footsteps or doors banging, and when she ventures into the corridor she finds no-one there. One of her staff members, a young man of around twenty, is now afraid to go into the cellar, which is not actually below ground but backs onto the bar and has outside access to the car park area. The incident which first alarmed him occurred one sunny, spring day in 2006, as he worked quietly on his own in the cellar. He thought he could hear voices whispering close by and soon experienced an unnerving sense of dread or terror. He could not explain why he suddenly felt so perturbed, but he did. On several occasions after that he reported hearing his name being called and when calling out a reply, expected to see the land-lady or another member of staff, but found he was quite alone. From that time on, he worked with the cellar door firmly held open, as the experience unnerved him so.

Local lady Sandra Valentine has worked as a cleaner at the Bell and Bottle for over ten years and has had numerous encounters. She tells of seeing a strange dark shape fleetingly as it rushed from one particu-lar part of the bar towards the front entrance – she was working alone in broad daylight and the shape appeared in the same area of the bar where the young phantom stable lad is often reported. She has been in the ladies toilets working and heard someone come in, only to look out and see no-one there at all. She tells the story of a 'helpful spirit' who seems to like to tidy up too, as one day when she was cleaning in the billiard room adjacent to the main bar she noticed a beer mat on the floor and made a mental note to pick it up later after she had

finished another of her jobs. When she returned to it minutes later, and still alone in the room, the beer mat had been carefully deposited on a nearby table. On one other occasion, Sandra and the assistant bar manager were behind the bar prior to opening time but at opposite ends and both heard a voice speaking aloud, which seemed to come from the restaurant area. Upon checking they found that there was in fact no living soul around other than they themselves.

Locals who have frequented the Bell and Bottle for many a year have reported phenomena too. One regular asked if the 'old man in the corner' was all right as he thought he looked extremely melancholy or ill, but upon looking back he found that the old man had disappeared. Psychics who have visited the pub have also picked up on this old gent – we can only speculate as to who he may be.

Local legends may hold a key to these paranormal phenomena at the inn, which is believed to be built upon an ancient site and many tell of the Bell and Bottle originally being an old farmstead of some kind. Some locals have heard stories of a young girl who was accidentally drowned in the pond which was once here, now no longer in existence, so she, along with the stable boy, makes *two* unfortunates who are rumoured to have lost their lives here. The girl's death could perhaps explain another auditory phenomenon that is often reported, that of a child playing or singing in the area to the left of the entrance.

Who or whatever haunts this old inn, there is no doubt there seems no logical explanation for the constant noises which current landlady Collette has to endure along the upstairs corridor in the dead of night, as she bravely tries to get a peaceful night's sleep!

The Wellington Inn, Preston City

The Wellington Inn in the heart of Preston's city centre has a reputation for housing the ghost of a murdered patron. The phantom drinker, who seems to have returned to his favourite 'haunt' or watering hole, makes his presence known by thrashing about making loud (drunken) noises. Several landlords – and -ladies – have heard his ranting in the dead of night after closing time and, following some research undertaken by a previous landlady, Christina Smith, in 1991, believe it to be one of two locals who drank here regularly in the early 1800s.

The story goes that the pair, who were good friends and lived locally in Avenham, got into an argument in 1839 over a one penny piece. The argument escalated into a street brawl as the two spilled out onto Glover Street. The fight apparently continued outside their homes

long after they had left the pub and culminated in one of the men stabbing the other, resulting in his subsequent untimely demise. Consequently, the guilty party was sentenced to many years hard labour. It is believed, however, that the unfortunate victim returns to the site of the argument, in an attempt to find the disputed coin. At the time of taking over the pub, Christina was told that there were unexplained noises heard in the pub after closing time, and particularly on the landing at night. Her dog had apparently barked at an unseen force in this area and in an attempt to appease the spirit of this poor soul, Christina, in her desperation, left a penny on the landing in the hope that he would simply leave.

However, it seems her attempts were in vain, as years later the same inexplicable loud noises were still being reported. Furthermore, first hand sightings, glasses smashing and even corkscrews shooting across the pub, have all been reported as 'normal everyday occurrences' at the Wellington to this day.

In November 2006 the current landlady Cheryl Holmes and her staff believed that this activity seemed to be escalating, as Lindsey Anders, a barmaid there, talked about recent paranormal activity: "A cork was left on the side of the bar and as a member of staff walked in behind the bar it just shot off the shelf onto the floor". This poltergeist incident was actually captured on CCTV which was running behind the bar at the time. Staff there also report seeing the apparition of someone who looks like a maid. She is often seen on the back stairs of the establishment, although no-one is sure who this might be. Cheryl also reports having seen some 'thing' go straight through the wall as she was walking up the stairs: "It's difficult to describe what it looked like as it moved very fast. I did manage to see its 'legs' striding quite quickly as it disappeared through the wall".

Niki Park, who has worked and lived on the premises for ten years, describes herself as 'quite sceptical usually'. However, she too has also seen this apparition; in fact she had to avoid it as she entered her bedroom one night and courteously moved out of its way, until she realised that it was not a real person, but rather something she later described as a dense, dark shadow. Niki's dog often refuses to go into the bedroom with her, instead cowering and growling at some unseen presence which perhaps only he can see or sense.

Caroline Fleming, a regular at the Wellington, says these recent phenomena are not new to the Wellington, as she has heard tales of this type before. Over the years she has been frequenting the Wellington, she has been told that there is the spirit of a man who haunts the cellar area of the lower floors, and she knows of previous staff members who would not venture down there alone due to the oppressive nature of the atmosphere and feelings of unease experienced there. A local electrician was working on the premises in broad daylight and told Niki: "There's a big, black shadow over there, have you got a ghost?" Landlord George has also seen a figure which he described as a cavalier type, rather large in stature, leaning casually against the beautiful old marble fire surround in the front of the bar area.

Another living regular at the Wellington believes she has actually caught the spectral visitor on film – well, mobile phone actually! Whilst taking a photograph of her boyfriend, Jamie Morton, in the pub, trainee beauty therapist Laura Wilkinson seems to have captured

some other entity as well. In the top right hand corner of the picture, next to Jamie's head, is a strange white mist which seems to look like a face.

Pete Bony, of the Paranormal Activity Research Team of Lancashire, says his group was invited to give their opinion on what it might be, and, whilst he tried to remain sceptical, he conceded that 'it could be related to the paranormal ... it looks like a face'. Pete and his team were so intrigued that they visited the pub in late 2006 to investigate further, using equipment such as EMF (Electro Magnetic Frequency) metres, and EVP (Electronic Voice Phenomena) recorders, both of which can sometimes assist in the recording of paranormal activity (though they were not originally designed for this purpose). A local reporter from the *Lancashire Evening Post*, Melanie Wallwork, complete with video camera, was also on hand to capture any ghostly activity, should it occur. The team also brought along with them psychic Marlene Bony, who was able to come up with the name 'Al' for one of the apparitions. They also appeared to be in the presence of 'Tom' in the cellar and believe him to be a drayman from the days when the Wellington was a coaching house. A 'Mrs Roberts', a housekeeper, was believed to roam the top floor, along with a small boy and another male, who may have been a doctor in attendance to this young, and apparently sick, child. Other departed souls were also reported as being present on this floor, which had been used as servant accommodation in the Victorian period. The night they investigated, they reported extreme cold chills and feelings of unease throughout several parts of the building. Whilst nothing substantial was found on film after the event (save for a few light anomalies, or orbs, as they are sometimes known), several loud knocks were recorded on the EVP recorders. Pete Bony can offer no 'logical' explanation for these.

Whoever these phantoms are, one seems to be making quite an effort to get themselves heard *and* seen, and has perhaps even succeeded in appearing on that most modern of inventions, the mobile phone!

The George Hotel, Preston City

In the bustling town centre of Preston stands the George Hotel in Church Street. Despite its rather ordinary external appearance, inside there lurks an unknown quantity that haunts this 300-year-old public house. Former landlords Tommy and Anne Harrison ran this popular watering hole in the late 1990s and eventually were driven out by the paranormal activity that dominated the establishment.

Within the first few weeks of taking over as landlords of the pub, they discovered an ancient gravestone in the cellar dating back to the time that the hotel was a coaching inn, sometime in the eighteenth century. The site upon which the George Hotel now stands is believed to have once been a burial ground dating back to the War of the Roses. Moreover, a famous battle during the Civil War of the early 1700s (the Battle of Preston and the skirmish at Brindle) was also uncomfortably close by, and it is said that many were buried here in unmarked graves. So where did the gravestone come from in the cellar? Paranormal expert Melanie Warren states in a series of *Ghost Hunters* featured on Discovery Channel TV that it was considered quite 'normal' for families in that time period to bury members of their family on their own plot of land – so the discovery of the tombstone was not unnatural in that respect.

However, Tommy soon became aware of an unnatural presence within the hotel which he could not explain, and it was one that left him feeling decidedly uncomfortable. But worse was to follow. One night he was awakened by extremely loud banging, like doors slamming shut – not just one door, but many doors, until the noise convinced him he was being burgled! Taking his trusty pooch with him, Tommy ventured forth down the stairs, whilst his wife Anne lay shuddering beneath the bedclothes in terror. He was stopped in his tracks by a sudden cold spot on the stairs and there in front of him stood a tall figure, dressed in what looked like Puritan apparel. The man shouted out 'Don't you ignore me!', then turned and walked purposefully down the remaining stairs and out of the door, slamming it loudly as he went. Tommy was now very afraid as he knew he had locked the door before retiring to bed that night, but he composed himself and continued down the stairs until he reached the door.

Tentatively his hand stretched out to try the door: it was locked, and from the inside.

Tommy's encounters do not end there, however, for as contractors began the replacement of some of the cobbles on the cellar floor there were further happenings. First a ring was found beneath one of the gravestones in the cellar with the inscription 'Robert Clay OB 28 Mar, 1786, aged 40', and then, over the next ten months, the aggressive ghostly figure manifested himself several times to both Anne and Tommy.

It is believed that any type of building work *can* trigger paranormal activity if a spirit is latent within the building, as it is believed that aggrieved spirits make themselves known if they take umbrage at the works that are being carried out, a sort of paranormal interior design clashing of wills – you like it, they don't! However, as events unfolded it seemed it was more than a simple 'objection', as it appeared that the spectre was in fact endeavouring to stop work on the cellar floor for a very good reason.

As time went on, Anne noticed that Tommy's mood changed and his behaviour become odder. Often he was heard by his wife and customers alike shouting as if in fierce confrontation with someone. Tommy says the phantom often appeared to him and insisted he get out of *his* place, whilst Tommy was likewise indignant that this was *his* pub and the spirit should leave, not him! Eventually, fearing for Tommy's sanity, his wife Anne suggested consulting a medium in order to discover who this was and what, if anything, the spirit wanted. Anne believed that every effort should be made to cleanse the hotel and move the spirit on to its rightful plane. Following a sitting with several mediums, Anne and Tommy discovered that the key to the mystery man and his appearances could be found in the cellar, where it was said that more gravestones could be uncovered, and even another ring. One séance conducted there culminated in the revelation that the ghost *was* in fact Robert Clay whose ring had been discovered by Tommy. But even more horrifically, it was this same Robert Clay who had abducted, abused and subsequently murdered two young girls and had hidden their bodies in a lower cellar beneath the existing one. After some further research it was discovered that there was indeed a second layer of cellar present, as depicted on some old maps. The mediums believed that it was Robert Clay's intention to stop Tommy from finding these bodies as he continued his restoration work on the cellar floor.

Undeterred, Tommy set out to discover as much as he could about Robert Clay, as he believed the answer to the dark phantom lay with him and the ring, which was in fact a bereavement ring – a ring which would have been worn by a close relative of the bereaved and not by the dead person themselves. Around the time that Robert Clay had died, 1786, there was only one Clay family living in Preston. Historical references showed that Robert Clay's father, John, was the governor of the house of correction, which was literally over the road from the George Hotel – a huge coincidence … or not? Sadly, no record of a Robert Clay could be found, but research undertaken by Tommy and Anne showed that two young children did go missing in the years before Clay's death and were never found. At that time, if a heinous crime was committed by a member of a well known or distinguished family, very often they would not only be written out of the family will and lose their inheritance, they would also be literally obliterated from the records, as if they had never existed at all. This is an interesting theory and could go some way towards explaining why no records exist of this Robert Clay, except of course, for the ring.

Within a year, Tommy and Anne had moved out, as Tommy's failing health was becoming a concern. Subsequent landlords who have taken over this public house – and there have been many, including Tony and Debbie Pickering who took over the running of the George in 1996 – have seen the dark and malevolent ghost. In fact during 1996, there were as many as five different tenancies in less than eight months! Some who left rather hurriedly complained of machines starting up on their own, glasses and other objects moving in the pub, loud inexplicable knockings, shouting coming from up the stairs, and worse of all, the Puritanically-clothed figure which had been seen in the main bedroom upstairs. But it is the cellar where his evil presence is felt the strongest. When Tommy left the George Hotel, he kept Robert Clay's bereavement ring and wore it constantly around his neck, believing that somehow, in some strange way, it would bring him luck. Tommy's final legacy before he left was to concrete over the entire cellar floor – had Robert Clay finally got his way?

The mystery of what may *still* lurk beneath the lower cellar still waits to be discovered ...

THE WHEATSHEAF INN, WOODPLUMPTON

A newspaper cutting dating back to October 1993 drew my attention to the Wheatsheaf Inn in the village of Woodplumpton, infamous home of 'Meg Shelton', a witch who was buried beneath a stone in the graveyard opposite the inn. However, this story relates not to a witch, but to a fireplace.

Dave McCormick took up the post of landlord in 1986 and like many other landlords was rightfully proud of his historic pub, so much so that he decided to record on film the various features of the building, including the large original stone fireplace in the main bar. After developing the pictures he decided to frame some of them and

display them around the inn, which seemed like the end of the story. Until seven years later.

In October 1993 Dave was asked by a customer one evening, "Have you seen the little girl in the picture?" Being a down-to-earth kind of guy his reply was "don't be so silly", but as he looked closely he could see that the image was definitely there. The sobering photograph appears to show a thirteen or fourteen year old girl in a purple dress polishing the brass around the fireplace, and watching over her is a medieval knight in a suit of armour. Puzzled regular Mrs Chris Massey said at the time, "it is very strange because it definitely wasn't there before".

Like so many other pubs and inns the Wheatsheaf has its fair share of ghoulish tales to chill the blood, one telling of a dark winter night in the mid 1980s when a terrified young motorist burst into the pub saying she had just knocked down an elderly lady outside. Upon investigation no trace of a body could be found. Could this have been the apparition of the witch Meg Sheldon? I decided to see if Veronica and I could shed any light on the case of the haunted fireplace and so we set off to investigate.

After examining the photograph Veronica sat down next to the fireplace, telling me, "there are two men standing here drinking ale, one has a clay pipe and is wearing a leather waistcoat and belt, he is a jovial chap, has long hair and I feel he is in charge of the inn, the name 'John' is given". I asked Cassie, the current landlady, if this made any sense. "Yes it does" she replied, "our cleaner has seen the form of a male figure sitting near the fireplace in the bay window and customers have experienced a 'cold spot' in the same place." Cassie also told me that the previous landlady had passed on a ghostly anecdote from years past, telling her that her granddaughter used to talk of an unseen friend that she used to play with. Others reported hearing small footsteps like that of a child in empty rooms. I asked Cassie if she was worried about living in a haunted inn and she replied that she believed in ghosts but was not bothered by their presence. A few moments later she added that she doesn't like being alone near the fireplace after dark!

THE RAILWAY INN, KIRKHAM

Prompted by a strange piece of video footage caught on a security camera I arranged to visit the Railway Inn, on the outskirts of Kirkham, with psychic Sybil Lucas-Brewer in December 1996. The footage, which I have seen, shows an anomalous figure in black surrounded by a contrasting white aura manifesting near the bar area and flying towards the camera and out of view. It was caught on 29 May 2005 and instigated a lot of interest from researchers all over the country. The video was also analysed by the local police, who were unable to explain it. Unseen at the time, the figure travels 15 yards in only a 3rd of a second, faster than any sentient person could possibly move.

When we met the landlord he told us that a team of ghost hunters had visited recently and one had seen a pair of disembodied legs run up a staircase. Unfortunately we didn't witness this curious manifestation ourselves, but we did encounter some strange cold spots which circled around Sybil and could not be logically explained. After spending several hours investigating the entire building and

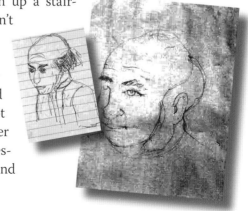

cellars, Sybil went into a trance and produced some psychic art which depicted an old man with a furrowed brow, thick bushy eyebrows and a bald head, telling us that she felt he was the spirit haunting the inn. I showed the picture to the landlord who reacted with a look of shock. Without explaining himself he told me he would be back in a moment and disappeared off into his flat upstairs. Minutes later he returned and produced a hand drawn sketch which had been created by another medium who had visited weeks earlier. Incredibly this also showed a bald headed old man with the same features Sybil had drawn! There was no clue as to his identity or why his restless ghost was haunting the inn until almost ten years later.

I revisited the building one summer evening in August 2005 with psychic Veronica Charles. She had never been to the inn before and I told her nothing of its history or haunted heritage. After coming out of the ladies toilets Veronica divulged a wealth of psychic information which she delivered in a matter of moments, so rapidly were the images and feelings filling her mind and body: "There is a man wearing a long dark cloak or trench coat here, he's looking at a watch and saying 'I'm Late' to himself. In his hand he is carrying a lantern and I feel he is connected to the railway outside". She continued: "I feel he met with a sudden death whilst crossing the track on a dark rainy night, the name Thomas Pilkington is ringing in my head."

So, is the spirit caught on camera in 2005 and drawn by two unconnected psychics really the ghost of a former rail worker who perhaps met with an untimely end? So far I have been unable to locate a record of a Thomas Pilkington, and yet the video footage and psychic drawings cannot be easily dismissed. But for now this fascinating old haunt still holds on to its secrets.

The Old Hob Inn, Bamber Bridge

Standing near to a busy highway the Old Hob Inn, built in 1616, is now a welcoming stopping place for weary travellers seeking fine food and ale, its open fire, rustic charm and mysterious history making this tavern a popular haunt for the living, as well as the dead.

Landlord Dave Adams Wilson told me that his first encounter with something supernatural at the pub was one evening around 12.30 p.m. He was preparing himself some sandwiches before retiring to bed and as he went to leave the kitchen he heard a kettle switch on in the adjoining bar area of the restaurant. Assuming that his wife had come down to make herself some coffee he was in no hurry to investigate, but when he returned to his living quarters upstairs minutes later, he found his wife fast asleep. Months later, in March 1999, he was spending the night alone in the building and had retired to bed with his two guard dogs in tow. He had not been asleep very long when he was awoken with a start by the sound of a door slamming so hard that he thought it must have come off its hinges, and his dogs had also been disturbed by the sound and were whimpering in the corner of the bedroom. The same thing happened again several weeks later, although on this second occasion the force was not quite as strong as the first, and during the encounter his wife heard the sound as well. They began to realise they were sharing their new pub with a visitor of the spectral variety.

The next incident occurred one lunch time as a group of three elderly customers were enjoying lunch in the main bar. David was on duty that day and had cause to leave the bar momentarily to collect something from the kitchen. As he arrived in the kitchen he heard something smash in the bar and rushed back to see what had happened, finding three bemused customers who informed him that a bottle of beer had levitated off a shelf behind the bar, flown across the room and smashed in the middle of the floor!

When I visited the pub with psychic medium Angela Borrows in March 2001, a pub regular told me of the time when he was watching football in the lower bar and was surprised to feel someone invisible digging him in the ribs. He was so scared by the incident that he left in the middle of the match!

A customer who claimed psychic abilities once told David that the inn was haunted by a friendly female spirit, and this certainly seems to fit in with the most famous sighting on record. Peter Terrell, a regular at the pub, relates the tale:

"It was around 10.30 p.m. one evening and I noticed a woman walk past the bar and enter the ladies loo. The strange thing was that minutes later she had not emerged and so we sent someone in to check on her – but the toilet was deserted. She had a 'normal' appearance, with modern day clothes and looked to be aged between 30 and 50 years."

I decided to investigate further and discovered, via Ann-Marie Houghton, a local journalist, that some years ago a middle-aged woman had come into the pub to meet someone after work, but had dropped dead in the main bar area. Could this explain the ghostly activity at the Hob Inn?

As I investigated this case further I was put in contact with another local, who does not wish to be named, who told me of a second ghost in the building. She said, "I know a girl who used to work behind the bar at the Hob. She told me that one Sunday night she was getting ready to lock up the building. Her husband had come to meet her and was waiting at the bar and as he looked through the archway to the lower bar he saw what he described as a tall man wearing a long trench coat walk across the room from left to right. He was very frightened by the experience and they left as quickly as they could."

So who is this second spirit presence that was witnessed that Sunday night? Could the answer lie in a ouija board experiment conducted by Angela and myself in the pub during an overnight investigation? We were contacted by the spirit of a man named 'William Faulkner', who claimed to be a blacksmith from the seventeenth century, and to have lived and died in the building. I have been unable to verify the name in local records but I did discover that part of the current building used to be a cottage – perhaps a blacksmith's cottage?

CHAPTER THREE

STATELY SPECTRES

WORDEN HALL, LEYLAND

To the south of Preston in an area of Leyland lies the tranquil Worden Park. Worden Park formed part of the estate which once belonged to the Farington family and it is here that they lived for centuries in relative splendour. The original estate was bought by Sir Henry Farington in 1534, for his son William, and it is said that the old Worden Hall (built around the early part of the fifteenth century) was part of an older manor house called Shaw Hall, which dated back to the thirteenth century.

Later, around 1715, the Farington family moved to an even grander domicile, an impressive home which became known as Worden Hall. This hall was improved upon and greatly enlarged in 1847 for James Nowell Farington, who had inherited the family estates in 1837. The famous Victorian architect Anthony Salvin was commissioned to re-design and build this new hall, and the gardens were also landscaped at this time by Salvin's brother-in-law, William Andrew Nesfield, who famously designed the gardens at Alton Towers and Kew.

The Farington family were in residence here up until 1947 when the last Farington died without issue. Sadly, a fire in 1941 had badly damaged almost all of the hall, so with no heirs and the building in a terribly dilapidated state, the remaining furniture, tapestries and fine art treasures were sold at a public sale in 1948. Leyland Urban District Council bought Worden Park and the remaining parts of the hall in November 1950 and opened it to the public on 18 June 1951.

The main part of the building was eventually demolished in the early 1960s, and now, sadly, only the Derby Wing, the oldest part of the

hall, remains intact. Overlooking what was once the formal garden, is a magnificent conservatory originally built in 1892, and alongside is the famous maze or puzzle garden. Other features of the park include a folly built as a romantic ruin with a water cascade and the existing doomed eighteenth-century ice house. Newer purpose-built facilities such as the adventure playground, miniature railway, crazy golf course, arboretum and garden for the partially sighted have been added in recent years.

It is here in this ancient and idyllic setting that South Ribble Borough Council run Worden Arts and Crafts Centre. The coffee shop and small craft units are housed in the old stable yard and are a popular visitor attraction. Sometimes, however, it would seem that other 'visitors' are in residence here too!

There have been many reported sightings and spooky goings-on in the Arts Centre, which is housed in the oldest remaining part of the hall – the Derby Wing, built in 1780. This paranormal activity manifests itself in several forms. Physical materialisations of a beautiful lady and an Edwardian-clothed gentleman are seen regularly. Phantom footsteps, whisperings, and 'unusual' poltergeist phenomena are just a few of the paranormal events at Worden Hall. Lights switch off and on at random, sounds of hustle and bustle are heard in what used to be the kitchen – could this be residual sounds of the original inhabitants and their staff, going about their daily duties? Staff here report the strangest poltergeist activity I have heard of yet, that of pot-washing! Apparently, when a member of staff leaves their washed cups and saucers on the draining board, they are often found later, back in the sink, ready to be washed again! Perhaps the 'servants' are continuing to fulfil their duties still!

Community Development Officer Jane Fletcher and her colleague Marilyn Deverill have personally witnessed this most bizarre of poltergeist behaviour. They also report seeing a tin lid from a well known sweet manufacturer literally fly across the room whilst they were all working at their desks one morning. Andrea Morris and her daughter Georgina, who both work in the centre's café, have become quite used to the shenanigans. Andrea Morris once sensed some presence in the doorway of a room where a conference/seminar was being held. She was sure that there was someone there, waiting for the right moment to come in, and that eventually this 'feeling' manifested itself into a lady in what Andrea later described as 'period costume'. She beckoned

for the lady to come in, and when she did not Andrea followed her into the next room, only to find that there was no-one there and the main entrance door was locked.

In June of 2006, a local group of students from Runshaw College got more than they bargained for when, whilst attempting to set up a mock séance as part of their media college project, discovered that in fact, someone other worldly *did* appear to be with them that night. James Entwistle, Georgina Morris and Rebecca McDermott all witnessed a cup move inexplicably without them touching it. A deep sigh was heard on film, although none of the students had made a sound. They also found to their terror that the door to the area they were in, previously locked to stop others entering during filming, was now open as they began to pack up and leave. Georgina, no stranger to these unearthly events, had witnessed such things before, as she worked part time in the centre's café: "I've seen some unexplainable things whilst I've been there, like the coffee machine pouring itself a cup and the commercial fridges turning themselves off. I'm in no doubt the place is haunted!"

Upstairs in the council offices men's voices are often heard talking and often a melancholy gentleman in Edwardian attire, complete with pocket watch, is seen watching over workers in the offices. Some feel his oppressive presence bearing down on them at work; others hear his voice in conversation with another man. Both Andrea and Michelle have heard these voices on frequent occasions. One cold dreary winter's evening at about 6 p.m., the voices seemed so real that the women, fearing that some people were still lingering behind after a meeting, went out into the corridor to inform them that they really should be locking up now and that they should leave. To their amazement, no-one was in the vicinity and at that time of night, just as they were about to leave, they felt decidedly unnerved. Michelle Allsopp, the Community Arts Officer there, tells the story of how she was about to leave one evening when she saw quite clearly the shape of a man leaning against the outside of the building in full view of the CCTV. She was quite bothered about this, being the last to leave the building, but as she watched the man, he literally disappeared before her eyes. She apparently left work in rather a hurry that night.

But it is not just the café and the offices which appear to have a haunting. The theatre is housed in what was once the old stable to the property. Ponies have actually been seen in this vicinity and often their whinnying is heard. Heavy footsteps are heard on the back stairs up to the dressing room of the theatre when no-one is there, and, oddly, an old musty smell seems to accompany this phenomenon.

At the time of writing a paranormal research group have visited Worden, as its haunting is fast becoming notorious in the local area. Following their overnight vigil in the haunted building, which was also videoed, they are convinced too that the centre is 'a hotbed of activity' (*Lancashire Evening Post*). They experienced fluctuations in temperature and light anomalies on camera. They also took part in table tilting and in a ouija board experiment to see if they could contact the spirits of the hall. The investigation team are convinced that the hauntings have something to do with the spirit of a maid named 'Phyllis', who was apparently killed when the fire destroyed the hall in 1941. Another spirit also made his presence known and goes by the name of 'Victor Farington', a previously unheard of member of the Farington family.

I myself was lucky enough to actually be privy to one aspect of this haunting as, one beautiful summer's day last year during our research for this book, Jason Karl, Veronica Charles (one of our mediums) and myself all shared the same paranormal experience, along with our guides for the day, Jane Fletcher and Marilyn Deverill. In one of the rooms off the office area where Jane and Marilyn work, as we were talking quite normally, I found myself feeling decidedly uncomfortable for no reason that I could pinpoint. Veronica had been picking up on several of the spirits of the hall as we explored the first floor and she too felt the same sense of unease and suggested that perhaps we had somebody following us round on our tour at this point! Veronica was soon sensing more and more, as she began to describe a beautiful lady who was associated with the hall. She also felt the presence of an Edwardian gentleman, dressed in fine clothes, stiff-collared white shirt and a walking stick. This gentleman seemed quite agitated when we began to talk of the beautiful lady and asked us "Not to speak about her!"

After we had been shown around the upstairs of the building and then out into the grounds, we were taken downstairs into what must have been the old kitchen of the original hall, as a huge fireplace domi-

nated what was now the conference room. As we lingered to look at the old historic records of the hall, two things amazed us. Firstly, the lady that Veronica had picked up on whilst we were upstairs in the offices was there in full view in an old newspaper article about the old hall and its former residents. Here she was, just as Veronica had described her upstairs, "a well respected and elegant lady with hat and fine clothing, a beautifully embroidered bustier drawn in at the waist … I feel there is a picture of her here somewhere in the hall".

As we excitedly discussed this lady and pondered more on her fate, we heard a loud knocking at one of the doors which leads to the courtyard/bar area. We laughed at the knocking and Veronica joked, "Sorry, you cannot come in, we're busy". And as Jane opened the door to the inner bar area, she was astounded to see that not only was there no-one there, but the inner door from the bar to this part of the building was firmly locked, meaning that no-one living could have knocked at that door, or even got into this enclosed area. We all felt the hairs stand up on the back of our necks as we realised that perhaps we had inadvertently told the ethereal visitor to go because we were 'busy'!

It was the perfect end to the day and as we left we marvelled at how many others may have experienced the same sort of paranormal activity in this once magnificent stately home.

ALSTON HALL, LONGRIDGE

Alston Hall, built in 1876, is situated in Longridge, approximately six miles east of Preston and is housed upon an ancient Anglo-Saxon site. The old village of Alston, situated in the picturesque Ribble Valley, originally came under the parish of Ribchester within the Amounderness One Hundred. Records show that the village was first referred to as 'Alston' in 1226, as 'Halleston' in 1246, and as 'Alfston' in 1250. The name is a derivative of the Old English words 'Ælf's', a person's name, and 'tûn', meaning 'village' or 'estate' – 'a village belonging to Ælf'.

Much of the surrounding land was owned by the de Hoghton family who held sway over this manor from as early as the thirteenth century up until the end of the eighteenth century. Alston Old Hall was built here at some time in this medieval period. Eventually, however, after non-payment of mortgages, the de Hoghton family lost the land and the old hall, thus ending the reign of generations of de Hoghtons as it passed to John Acheron Nelson of Airburst Hall, Withington. On his death in October 1822, the Alston Hall Estate was sold to a Mr Edward Riddell of Cheeseburn Grange, Northumberland, who leased it to Edmund Sager, who became a resident at the old hall for many years whilst farming the land here. Alston Old Hall still stands here at the lower end of Alston Lane and past building work does reveal the hall's medieval origins.

Eventually, through the death of the landowner Mr Riddell, the estate once again came up for auction and it passed to Frank Chadwick of Grimsargh for the princely sum of £7,400 in 1868. In 1873, the estate was sold again by the son of Frank Chadwick – Francis Chadwick – to John Mercer, a colliery owner whose forebears had lived and made their fortune for generations in Lancashire. It was he who built the 'new' Alston Hall on the site we see it on today. Sadly, the Mercers seemed to have been dogged with bad luck. On 3 September 1864, John Mercer's brother William Mercer died in a tragic road accident as a horse drawn carriage overturned and flung out its occupants, causing serious and ultimately fatal head injuries to William. Then just four days later, on the day after his brother's funeral, John's wife Elizabeth died suddenly at home.

John remarried two years later and he and his new wife Helen intended that the new Alston Hall be their family home. Unfortunately, their second son William died in 1874 at the tender age of nine months and never saw the completion of the hall. Following the death of his first son in 1876, also named John and aged only four years of age, John Mercer senior is said to have cursed every stone in the house, wishing it to "fall into the river". Yet despite the tragic events at the time the new house was being built, he continued to live and entertain there until his death in 1893.

Currently owned by Lancashire County Council, Alston Hall is now an adult educational college offering courses which specialise in creative and self development. The hall has a typical Victorian façade and has undergone many incarnations under previous owners. Now, although modernised to accommodate its new role as a college, some wonderful original architectural features remain inside – along with some other worldly aspects too!

There are many visitors to Alston Hall; many come here to take part in various adult courses – the emphasis being on learning and perhaps taking away some new skill or attribute which they may not have had previously. But some people may take away far more than they bargained for, as in the case of David Summerville from Singleton near Blackpool. David described the hall as having an 'atmosphere', which he now believes to be of a paranormal kind. And he is not alone, as several people, visitors and teachers alike, have sensed a ghostly presence in the area which is believed to have once housed the original stables and outbuildings. Some have seen dark shadowy forms and heard voices, only to find that they are, in fact, alone in that part of the building. Phantom footsteps are often heard in dark corridors, long after most people have left. Doors bang and handles are turned, although no living hand seems to be manipulating them. When challenged by a 'Come in' no earthly presence appears. These paranormal occurrences apparently continue up to this day.

In David's case, as a qualified teacher and artist, he came here in the mid 1970s and for five years he taught courses in art and design, specialising in pottery classes for beginners and the advanced alike. At that time, the pottery and art department was situated on the upper floor of these old outbuildings. It was housed in a long room which could be reached by a series of old wooden stairs. As the residential teacher, David found himself, more often than not, working long days, and on many occasions late into the night in an attempt to keep the kiln constantly fired. Sometimes, feeling too tired to move, he would even catch up on his sleep sitting in front of the fired kiln, enjoying the warmth, peace and quiet. As David himself says, "I didn't mind as I was fit and in my early twenties. My room with its comfortable bed and shower in the hall was rarely used!"

One night, in the early hours, on such a night as this, he was 'resting' when he heard heavy footsteps downstairs walking along the corridor which led to the flight of wooden stairs up to the pottery. Thinking that one of his students was about to sit with the firing kiln, giving him a few hours in his soft, and so far neglected, bed, he arose from his cosy spot and went to the top of the wooden stairs to greet them. He stopped and waited and was at once greeted by a chill which went through his very bones. As he peered into the darkness, looking down towards the foot of the stairs, and listened intently as he heard the sound of purposeful footsteps on each wooden step coming directly towards him. For some seconds he continued to scan the stairs, his eyes now accustomed to the shift from light to pitch black. He realised that the footsteps were growing increasingly louder as they climbed higher towards him, yet still he could not see anyone approaching. To his total amazement, the footsteps, now extremely loud, stopped directly in front of him and to his horror he realised that there was not a living soul in sight! At the same time, that same chill he had first felt on his approach to the staircase was with him once more. The heightened sense of dread was almost too much to bear as he called out, "Hello, anybody there?" After what seemed like an age, but was probably only a minute or two, he called out once more – no response! Almost in a daze, David stood there silently now at the top of the old wooden stairs and contemplated long and hard what he should do next, eventually deciding that his best bet would be to pack up, switch off the kiln and go immediately to his own comfortable bed, but not before smoking several cigarettes in quick succession to calm his nerves! As he locked up and double checked the building he was not really comforted by the knowledge that there was, in fact, no-one else in the building save for himself.

Years later, David still retells this tale to others and remembers vividly the experience as if it were only yesterday. As he says in his own words: "Was I tired, was my imagination working overtime? Whatever the answer, I firmly believe that something came to see what was going on in their stable that night and I for one will never forget it!"

Samlesbury Hall, Samlesbury

Nestling halfway between Preston and Blackburn lies the ancient and historic Samlesbury Hall. The original country seat of the Southworth family, it was erected following orders from Gilbert de Southworth in 1325. Subsequent generations added to the original Great Hall creating the stately residence seen today. After being stripped of everything of value and heading for demolition in the 1920s it was rescued by a board of trustees who still manage the daily operations, opening it to visitors and showcasing in a number of rooms a variety of antiques which are available for purchase.

Mystery and charm combine at Samlesbury Hall, and tales of its most infamous ghost the 'White Lady' are surrounded by whispers of murder, suicide and intrigue. Perhaps one of Lancashire's most well documented phantoms, I opened a case on my files in May 1996 to examine the evidence for what has become a controversial story.

Legend has it that the White Lady is the melancholic manifestation of Dorothy Southworth, alleged daughter of Sir John Southworth who was High Sheriff of Lancashire in 1562. She became acquainted with a dashing young knight from nearby Hoghton Tower, but Sir John was deeply against this union and forbade his daughter from seeing her beau. The de Hoghton family had denounced Roman Catholicism in favour of the Protestant faith and Sir John, adamantly Catholic, was furious that Dorothy would consider a Protestant for a husband. Forced into secrecy the two continued their courtship, meeting each evening in a leafy arbour in the grounds of the hall. It wasn't long before plans for a covert elopement were underway, but fate was not on their side and family values were to wreak a terrible toll on this young love affair. Concealed within a thicket nearby, Dorothy's brother overheard the two planning their escape and reported their intentions back to his father. Enraged, Sir John instructed his son to lie in

wait at the appropriate time and to scare away the young de Hoghton once and for all. On the night in question Dorothy watched from her bedroom as her suitor and his companion crossed swords with her brother, their blades flashing in the moonlight until blood stained the ground and three dead bodies littered the arbour. The 'scare' had gone too far and de Hoghton, plus his two companions, had paid a terrible price.

It is here that the legend starts to vary depending on the account you read; one says that the heartbroken Dorothy was so distraught that she threw herself out of the window, killing herself in the act and joining her love in eternity. Another version says Sir John was so angered by her behaviour that he vowed never to set eyes on her again and banished her to a convent in France where she eventually went mad. Either way the story is entangled with even further speculation as no actual record of Dorothy ever existing has been found. Some suggest all mention of her was obliterated intentionally by Sir John, others say the story is a fabrication created to deter close inspection of the hall when it was used for illegal Catholic masses in the 1500s.

Whether the story is an accurate depiction of events, or an amalgamation of heresay and deliberate fraud, can never be proved, but what cannot be disputed are the sightings of a ghostly woman which have been reported over and over again. The earliest reference to the White Lady comes from a book published in 1875 which relates the popular legend of the doomed elopement. In 1878 a retired Colonel reported that he heard a "bitter sobbing" whilst staying at the hall and was unable to find any natural cause. On February 7th of the same year a Mr Sharples who was employed at the house reported that he and fellow workman Jacob Baron were excavating a drain and inadvertently broke into a sealed vault on the outskirts of the garden wall. Upon inspection the remains of three human bodies were seen, but quickly decomposed as the fresh air rushed in. The next recorded appearance was 47 years later in 1925 when two ladies, requiring milk from a nearby farmhouse named 'Collin's Bridge', watched in awe as a shadowy woman who they described as "slightly built with flowing hair and dressed all in white" manifested in front of them while they awaited their provisions. Subsequently razed to the ground this building no longer exists. Her next documented appearance was on January

10th 1940 at 11.45 p.m. Caretaker Edward Smith and his companion had been lying in wait for three nights hoping to see the ghost, and their wish was granted when a grey wraith-like form passed silently along the Long Gallery in front of them. Halting momentarily at the fireplace on the western wall she then proceeded to dissolve away as they watched in awe. Two years later on 16 September 1942 two gentleman taking the night air encountered the phantom as they walked in the grounds. They described "something uncannily sinister" about her presence and one collapsed on the drive as she followed them, the other running for help. So disturbed was the gentleman by the experience that he was detained in hospital for several days; the other also took some time to recover from the curious encounter. She appeared again six years later when a play was being performed at the hall in October 1948. Several cast members watched a lady dressed in white walk past their dressing room window, assuming her to be one of them; upon checking they realised they were all accounted for inside. 1948 was a record year for the ghost as she was seen again, this time on two occasions in the same night by different people. The first was a bus driver who, having seen a lady in a light-coloured coat standing near the bus stop outside the hall, assumed she was waiting to be picked up. He dutifully stopped the late night bus and opened the door and the conductor looked strangely at him. "Why have you stopped?", he asked. The driver related that he had seen a lady waiting, yet the conductor had seen no-one and angrily told him to drive on. Later the same evening a couple walking their dog on nearby Nab's Lane watched as a "lady in a light-coloured mackintosh" brushed swiftly and silently past them – walking right through their dog's lead! It wasn't until 1962 that the next record of the White Lady was written, this time as seen by Author Mr G. F. Eastwood, who encountered the spectre in the archery field in the grounds of the hall.

With these eight famous accounts of the same sighting and the discovery of three human skeletons in 1878 the evidence goes a long way towards substantiating the reality of a haunting at Samlesbury, but I was keen to try to find some contemporary evidence so I arranged to visit the hall with Veronica Charles in September 2005.

Sharon Jones, director of the trust which own the hall, met us in the entrance hall where she told us of her own ghostly encounter:

"It was very late one night after a function in February 2004. We had just said good night to the last guests and I was sitting by the fire in the Great Hall with the other staff winding down before going home. Suddenly I shot up from my seat having felt hot wax fall onto my head. It was a definite tactile feeling but there were no lighted candles near me at the time! I didn't feel frightened, more fascinated,

although everyone else joked that Dorothy had stroked my hair and I have never heard the last of it since. We also have a trustee who was invited to walk around the hall by himself when he first visited here years ago. When he approached the parlour door it flew violently open in front of him – even though usually this door has a tendency to stick and is very difficult to open."

Captivated by this new tale I thanked Sharon and Veronica and I made our way to the chapel. Goosebumps crept across Veronica's arms as we walked around the room: "There are three gentlemen here and a lady who is connected to one of them," she stated. I wondered to myself if these could be Dorothy, her lover and his two companions who had been murdered centuries earlier. Veronica looked further into her psychic vision: "the woman has been judged in this room, wrongly accused. There is a connection with a betrothal and opposing religious faiths. Lies and deception. I am also being shown a silver sword and an amulet." I was amazed by this testimony which seemed to tie in with the popular legend of Dorothy and her young knight. Everything Veronica had seen made sense except for the amulet; perhaps that is yet to be found. Watching from the sidelines Sharon explained that the three skeletons had been discovered beneath the ground just outside the walls of the room in which we were standing. Spurred on by this initial success we retraced our steps to the entrance hall.

We were introduced to Julie, one of the hall's guides, who proceeded to share some of the stories she had been told over the years working at the old manor house:

"Many visitors have told me of curious encounters they have had whilst visiting the house. The most recent was during September 2005 when a visitor was coming down the staircase and felt suddenly that they should move to the side to allow someone to pass them. They told me that they had felt they would have been knocked over by the force if they had not moved out of the way – yet there was nothing to be seen!"

Julie continued, telling me that most sightings of the ghost take place during the month of August and that a photograph taken in the entrance hall by an American visitor had shown the curious image of a coffin in front of the fireplace, even though no such thing had been in the vicinity at the time.

Leaving Julie to her duties we explored the Great Hall and subsequently the Long Gallery. In each room Veronica told me that we were "being watched and observed" by unseen eyes, but it wasn't until we reached the Priest's Room that we encountered our next visitation. "There is a man in a cream robe holding a rosary – clearly a priest" said Veronica. "He is pacing up and down and praying – he knows he is going to die, it is as if he is waiting for the inevitable to happen." I assumed she was sensing something connected to the hidden priest hide which is next to the room we were standing in. It is a place where Catholic priests hid from the authorities during the times of Catholic persecution.

After exploring the rest of the antique-filled rooms we enjoyed a superb home cooked lunch at the hall and mused on the White Lady's apparent commercialisation by the trust, who are now offering evening ghost hunts to the public. It seems she made her dislike felt during one such event when a freak wind from nowhere blew down the tree which marked the spot where the remains of her lover had been found way back in 1878.

HOGHTON TOWER, HOGHTON

The hauntingly beautiful Hoghton Tower stands eminently atop a mighty crag, surveying the land for miles around. Built in 1565 it is now the country seat of Sir Bernard de Hoghton, BT, who perhaps not surprisingly shares this baronial mansion with a variety of other worldly inhabitants.

The famed – and haunted – Banqueting Hall is renowned for being where a joint of beef was given the name 'Sirloin' when King James 1st knighted it 'Sir Loin of Beef' on August 17th 1617. It is now part of the tour which thousands of visitors enjoy when the house is opened to the public every year.

When I first approached the owners of the tower in 1996 to ask if I could visit along with medium Sybil Lucas-Brewer my request was met with interest, and so on a blustery Monday in March of that year we drove up the narrow drive towards the ominous gateway of the Tower and were greeted enthusiastically, if somewhat nervously, by guide Christine Daniels.

As we explored the vast rooms, corridors and passageways we felt as if we were not alone in the Tower, almost as if unseen eyes were watching us from the shadows. Our first stop for investigation was the notorious East Wing which is closed from public view and from where strange noises emanate during the hours of darkness. We climbed the ancient oak staircase and Christine unlocked the door to the East Wing, and as we paused at the top Sybil picked up the psychic vibration of a gentleman who she said was watching us. Christine verified that the heavy footsteps of a man are often heard in the area, even though there is no-one around to account for them. Our conversation was disturbed by the sound of heavy furniture being moved around in the room below us, which Christine told us was due to the workman scheduled for duty that morning. Relieved, we explored the various rooms which are so rarely inhabited by the living and Christine told me an anecdote of a spectral event noted in the records of the Tower's past "when the 'Gallows Room' was finally unlocked after being abandoned by decades and a curious find was discovered. The floors were all covered with inches of thick dust but the windowsills were all completely dust free, as if they had been regularly cleaned."

After Sybil had connected with several psychic memories of past eras we decided to leave the East Wing and begin a tour of the main house, beginning with the Guinea Room.

We stood in the gloomy chamber in silence, Sybil trying to connect with any spectral presence which may be hiding, when suddenly the sound of a door latch was heard from the corridor next to us. "That's strange," Christine commented, continuing, "the doors all have door knobs; there are no latches as there would have been in the past." Moments later we found ourselves in the presence of one of the Tower's ghostly residents as we all heard the definite sound of slow footsteps approaching us along the corridor. Sybil and I looked at each other, wandering what might happen next whilst Christine huddled close to Sybil, hoping for some protection! When the sound had stopped a few moments later I examined the corridor for possible explanations, but there were none to be found. The Tower was closed to the public on that day so there was no-one around, and besides, the floor is covered with a deep pile carpet on that corridor, but the footsteps we heard were on bare floorboards.

By now Sybil and I were very excited by the prospect of what else might occur on that haunted morning at Hoghton. Christine, on the other hand, was becoming increasingly nervous and required a little re-assurance from Sybil that we were in no danger. Our next stop was the State Bedroom and as we entered Sybil said, "There is a powerful male spirit here, he is called 'Sir John' and he is indicating that he sits on a chair in this room". Christine confirmed that the cleaners often find that after they have plumped up the cushions on the chair and settee in this bedroom they return to find that they have been depressed, as if someone has been sitting on them. As we inspected the furniture the cushions did indeed look as if someone had been sitting on them recently, which Christine said was impossible as the cleaners had been the previous afternoon and we were the first people to enter the room since. Another incident which was reported in this chamber was the horrible sound of loud groaning, as if someone was dying, and this was heard one evening when the room was empty.

We left the State Bedroom and made for the Ball Room. It was in this room years ago that Sir James de Hoghton had a strange encounter with his Pekinese dog and Siamese cat. The dog started barking and running around in a circle whilst the cat, with its tail bolt upright, walked in a tight circle as if around a persons leg. As soon as we crossed the threshold Sybil was in contact with the spirits: "a lady with a very large hat is here, she is wearing a grey dress covered in beautiful lace and is tapping her sleeve impatiently with a glove, waiting for the dance to end". Christine told us that a sighting of this ghost, along with a second, was reported by an ex-administrator at the Tower who particularly noted the 'big hats' the spectres seemed to be wearing. Flowers have also been taken out of a vase on a table in this room, as if some ghostly presence disapproves of them. Could this behaviour be blamed on another ghost which has been seen in the room? During a recent tour of the house it was reported that a visitor witnessed a sighting of spectral children dancing around the room as if taking part in some kind of celebration. Sybil added that she could feel the presence of a young girl in a yellow dress dancing near to the fireplace; she was a blissfully happy spirit, unaware that she had passed on from this life.

In the King's Ante Chamber Sybil encountered "a young man sitting cross legged, smoking by the fire". She said she felt he had returned from service and described his hairstyle as "greased down tightly". Christine took us immediately to the bottom of the King's Stairs to show us a picture of Major Adams, who served in the army and loved his home, this house, dearly. The smell of his pipe smoke has been reported many times and his ghost has been sighted standing in a red smoking jacket at the bottom of the staircase.

We had been fortunate – or unfortunate in Christine's opinion – to witness several glimpses of psychic activity at the Tower that morning and Sybil's energy was running out, but before we left Christine insisted on taking us to the Banqueting Hall. As we made our way to the Hall Christine told us more of the building's haunted history, informing us of the ghost of a young girl which had been seen in the King's Hall, and how eleven people from a Sunday school once watched a ghost at the north entrance thinking it was a special effect put on for the visitors! The current Lord de Hoghton apparently shares his private quarters with a poltergeist who moved a plate of spaghetti eighteen inches whilst the room was enveloped in an unnerving silence. The silence was then broken by phantom footsteps from the room above. Tales of ghosts in the gardens include a lady in a white lace dress with a parasol, accompanying a young girl aged around six or seven, and a groundsman who has heard someone walking on some gravel when the area was deserted. Back in the Tower, workers remember the tale of a gale force wind which rushed through the building banging doors in its wake – even though it was a still, hot summer's day outside! The ghosts of this ancient house clearly dislike being disturbed and on one

occasion they turned off the mains water to the building in the middle of a special function, and at other times they have triggered the fire alarms for no apparent reason.

As we entered the vast Banqueting Hall Sybil sparked into life: "The energies here are very strong, this must be the most haunted area of the Tower," she said. Christine laughed, telling us she was right. Records tell of the sighting of a girl with blonde hair in ringlets and the strange figure of a ghostly woman in a deep green velvet dress who watches the activities below from the Minstrel's Gallery. Reports of this phantom date back to the Victorian era and many guides who work at the Tower today have felt her unseen presence. She is thought to be the wraith of Ann de Hoghton, whose unlucky suitor was shot dead on the eve of their planned elopement. As punishment for her involvement with a man her family considered to be unsuitable, she was sent to a nunnery where she spent the rest of her life. Her sad forlorn spirit is now the Tower's most prevalent phantom, still mourning the terrible loss of her earthly lover. Other reports tell of a different woman who has been seen sitting on the Gallery sewing, and has faded away when looked at.

Christine lead us up a small staircase and onto the Gallery, which leads to the Ladies' Withdrawing Room, originally a gentleman's study, where books have been known to move around of their own accord.

Here Sybil found the spirit of a large dog sleeping by the fireplace. Christine confirmed that one of the gentleman who used this room had kept gun dogs and this was possibly why Sybil had seen the animal. I found an interesting story concerning this room in my archives at the Ghost Research Foundation. The late Sir Cuthbert de Hoghton was writing a letter late one evening when suddenly loud laughter filled the air and he heard the rustle of silk, like that of a heavy-skirted figure close beside him which he felt was looking over his shoulder to see what he was writing. Rather than scare him the incident intrigued him and he often spent time in the room hoping the spectre would return, which it never did.

As we made our way back to the administrator's office we visited the Tudor well where it is said dogs react in strange ways, and then down into the tunnels which run beneath the house, allowing servants to move around unnoticed in times past. It was as we began to descend the steps into the first tunnel that Sybil sensed a man rushing towards us "Look out!", she cried, as I felt a cold rush of air sweep past me, touching Christine as it went. It would be an understatement to say that Christine was petrified by this brush with the icy touch of the unknown and we proceeded straight back to the office to calm her down.

After a well-deserved drink to steady Christine's nerves we concluded that our visit had been most productive and thanked Eileen for allowing us to investigate. Just as we were preparing to leave I asked if the workmen were still in the building as I wanted to take some photographs. "Oh they didn't come today after all," said Eileen, "there's no-one in the building but us!"

PARK HALL, CHARNOCK RICHARD

Park Hall leisure facility, including the children's theme park Camelot, may seem an unlikely venue for a ghostly sighting, and yet for some decades now there have been some well documented instances. Indeed, behind the modern facade of Park Hall there lies much history, myth and legend. The Hall has a chequered and sometimes unsubstantiated past, but ghost stories travel well by word of mouth. Tales of wandering monks, a love struck lady, a persecuted family priest even, all add to the rich tapestry which makes up this fascinating place.

The association with monks is believed to originate in several legends, including the tale of St Cuthbert whose body was dramatically moved from its original resting place in the safe haven of Lindisfarne, across the mainland, and at one point was hidden in dense woodland where Park Hall now stands, in order to preserve the remains of the saint and his relics. The local legend, passed down through the centuries, is that this was where Benedictine monks later built their monastery, although the site has never been subject to full archaeological exploration so the story remains unsubstantiated. That said, huge red sandstone boulders are littered around the place and the older parts of Park Hall itself do contain this stone. A small-scale excavation took place during the renovations and extension of Park Hall in the 1970s and some stone foundations were unearthed.

Following the Norman invasion, around 1086, much of the land was given off to the local lords as a reward for their assistance in the Norman Conquest. One of these Knights, Sir Henry de Lea, was given a half share of this land by William Banastre, apparently in return for a favour. It was upon this land that Sir Henry built his original manor house which became known as Park Hall – 'The hall in the beautiful parkland'. The other half of the land was owned by Richard de Charnock, hence the later name of Charnock Richard for this location.

In the thirteenth century another Henry de Lea, the High Sheriff of the County of Lancashire, was granted by Royal Charter the right to hold a weekly market here on Fridays and on the Feast of St Botulph, a three day fair. This then established Charnock Richard as a good place to settle and within thirty years or so the region which we now know as Lancashire became more heavily populated. During Edward II's reign, Sir Henry aligned himself with Sir Adam de Banastre in the 'Banastre Rebellion' of 1315 against Thomas, Earl of Lancaster. After this insurgence failed, both men were beheaded on nearby Leyland Moor. Through the marriage of his widowed heiress, his estates eventually passed into the de Hoghton's hands. As committed Catholics, the de Hoghtons sheltered many priests in the secluded stone mansion that was old Park Hall, and down through the centuries more recent residents for whom the hall was also a family home still recount tales of uncovered priest hides, and of the ghostly spectres seen within its walls and in the grounds.

In the early 1970s, John Rigby, a local businessman, took over the running and renovation of Park Hall. It is during this renovation period that so many 'ghost stories' were documented. He tells one story of a cleaning lady who, whilst working in the Dungeon Bar in the recently built banqueting hall, fled the building screaming after having seen a man hanging from the rafters. She later described him as "an old man with a beard and dressed in old robes". Others reported feeling a sense of unease in this part of the Hall, as if someone was watching them. Alec Price, in his book on Park Hall, *From A Saint To A King: The History of Park Hall, Charnock Richard*, is informed that this was an area of the Hall where foundations were discovered, believed to be dating back to pre-Norman times.

It was also in the banqueting hall that some rather unusual poltergeist activity seems to have occurred. The housekeeping department of the hotel was getting ready to set up for a wedding the next day, everything had been set out ready for the bridal party, tables dressed, cutlery and glassware set out and even the cake had been put on its stand. The head housekeeper locked up and went home, taking the keys with her as normal, knowing she would be first in the next day. The following morning, as she unlocked the banqueting hall door and stepped inside, she was completely amazed to see that every single thing that she had set up had been very carefully moved to the stage in the hall and the tables had been set up for a medieval feast!

Another lady who also worked here during that time said she had an unnerving experience as she arrived for work one morning. As usual, she entered through reception then passed through the restaurant and up the stairs to the cabaret lounge. As she passed along this narrow corridor next to the dressing rooms, out of the corner of her eye she noticed someone standing at the top of the stairs. She said 'Good Morning' to them and carried on her way. When she went back down to reception, she remarked to the girl there that it was very early (7.30 a.m.) for someone to be in already starting rehearsals. When the receptionist asked her what she meant she said she had just seen someone in what appeared to be fancy dress, a monk's habit to be exact, just standing silently by the dressing rooms. The receptionist informed her that there were certainly no rehearsals taking place at this time, and exclaimed: "You've see a ghost!" Although not frightened by it, she did wonder as time went by what it was she *did* see!

An unnerving paranormal experience occurred in another part of the hotel, this time much more frightening for the participant, when a local builder working with a team of men on the redevelopment of the hotel in the 1970s believed he felt a ghost pass right through him whilst working late one night. The team of builders was working round the clock to get the job finished on time, sometimes working well into the night, as needs must. As the men were enjoying their late tea break one evening around 7 p.m., they wondered where one of their number had disappeared to, as this night he did not come down to join them as usual. They even went so far as to look for him, finding in his work place his jacket and his tools, but not a sign of him anywhere. When he arrived at work the next day he asked one of the men to go and fetch his things, stating that he would not go in there himself. Mr Rigby, the then owner, was most perturbed as to why he was refusing to carry on working and asked the site foreman to have a quiet word with him. Now builders are not generally given to indulging in flights of fancy, stereotypically being large, burly, no-nonsense types. The story goes that the man was working outside one of the rooms which was being renovated and as he opened the door to the room and went in 'something' walked towards him with great sense of purpose, passing right through him and out of the room, slamming the door as 'they' went. As it passed through him it chilled him to the bone. As you can imagine, such an experience was rather unsettling to say the least. He turned quickly in an effort to flee and tried the door handle, but found that he could not get out. He panicked and was so desperate to get out of there that he escaped through an open window and literally ran off absolutely terrified! Despite several attempts at recreating the 'locked door' scenario, the foreman and Mr Rigby could not do so.

A Mr George Few of Leyland owned and resided here for over forty years during the sixties and early seventies, and during that time he and his family experienced many paranormal happenings. The phantoms, random knockings, whispering voices and other curious and unexplained noises heard in and around the hall gave rise to the family joke of 'Micky the Monk, looking for his lost lady love'.

But it is the phenomenon of the 'lost lady' or the 'white lady of the lake' that is the most seen. This local story has two quite differing time periods at its core. Some believe that the 'real' story goes back to the times that the monks were quarrying stone here many hundreds of years ago, apparently when they built a monastery on this ancient site.

Others believe that it is in fact a priest who is seen in connection with the lost lady of the lake, as it is not only monks who are believed to have been here, for in the turbulent Elizabethan period and beyond the de Hoghton family *did* shelter priests. Two legends have sprung up therefore, one suggesting a monk, the other a priest. Either way, the main story which surrounds our next well known spectre remains the same.

The story goes that a young maiden, having fallen in love with and found herself pregnant to one of these religious men, was so sick at heart with her love for him, and knowing that their love was both illicit and unholy, that she threw herself into the lake and drowned. Many have seen her and the monk/priest and speculate that their tortured souls still linger here as penance for their crime.

Several local policemen whilst patrolling their beat on foot and by bicycle have reportedly seeing her rising gracefully out of the water – all have said she is in fact a beautiful sight to behold. Not quite what one would expect of a ghostly visitation, but this one seems somehow surrounded by an ethereal bright light which appears to emanate from within her. During the winter of 1967, on a cold January day, Mr Few, his wife and daughter and a member of the staff from the hotel, all saw the apparition together at the same time. Mr Few and his wife, who lived in the front of the old Hall, first saw the strange and haunting figure apparently rising up out of the lake amidst the eerie morning mist, whilst they were looking out of their bedroom window. They quickly summoned the others who verified that the ghostly white figure of a woman could indeed be seen in the middle of the lake. Mr Few rushed downstairs in an attempt to gain a closer look at this vision, whom they later described as "a beautiful creature," but upon reaching the water's edge, to his astonishment he saw her literally disintegrate in front of his eyes. According to George Few, this sighting became a regular occurrence every twelve months at this exact same time.

One can only speculate as to whether this was the actual time of year that she met her demise. Perhaps she still looks for him in this place where she eventually took her own life – a place where the monks gouged out their stone to build their monastery, or where the persecuted priests may have often walked in quiet solemnity, and perhaps this was where the two lovers met.

Jimmy Longton, a well known local dowser, believes that many more spirits may haunt this ancient site, six to be exact – look out for them next time you visit!

HAIGHTON MANOR, HAIGHTON

After driving past a sign to Haighton Manor on my travels in search of haunted locales for this book, I was intrigued to find out more about this little known gem which stands to the north of the city of Preston. There has been a habitation on this site since 1066 and it is rumoured that Oliver Cromwell was once a house guest here. Today the building has been converted into a luxury country house hotel and is a popular haunt for locals, tourists and business people wishing to stay off the beaten track. I decided to take Veronica for a visit one September afternoon in 2005 in the hope that we would find some trace of its past, and perhaps even a ghost in its present.

Upon arrival we were met by the newly appointed hotel manager Nicola White, who enthusiastically showed us around the upstairs bedrooms and public areas of the manor. Veronica stopped half way along an upstairs corridor and informed us, "there is a man here, he looks like a farrier, and there are horses too". "That makes sense because this area overlooked the stables in years past," confirmed Nicola. We waited a few minutes in case Veronica was able to pick up any further information but none was forthcoming, so we made our way back downstairs and into the dining room. "There is a presence here, it's very faint and doesn't want to be found, and he's hiding from me," Veronica said as she entered the room, staring intently at the large stone fireplace. "He's here, by the fireplace, do you know of anyone who has seen a ghost in this area?" she asked. Nicola, a self confessed believer, confirmed that the dining room was indeed the 'haunted' room in the manor and that her predecessor had endured a night of haunting when she once slept on a sofa in front of the fireplace in the chamber. Years ago the room was a lounge and reports of moving cushions and drinks coasters had been passed on to Nicola when she took on her new role. Cutlery has also been known to move of its own volition in recent times when the space has been used as a dining room. "I can see him now, he's coming a little closer," said Veronica. "This spirit is a very small man, wearing a floppy hat and bent over in pain, he is very faint and I feel that we should not force him to communicate against his wishes." With that Veronica closed the link with this shy soul and we left the manor wondering why he still lingers there, unable or unwilling to rest. Who he was, and why he refused to share his story with us, is a mystery; perhaps one day we will return and contact once again the reticent ghost of Haighton Manor.

CHAPTER FOUR

SPOOKS IN STORE

THE PLAYHOUSE THEATRE, PRESTON CITY

It is a cliche that theatres are frequently credited with being haunted, but often this is with very good reason. One such theatrical establishment has been at the heart of Preston's haunted heritage for some years – the historic Playhouse Theatre on Market Street.

As with many haunted theatres, there is a rich history dating back centuries. The structure we now know as the Playhouse Theatre, built in 1849, stands proudly on the site of a much more ancient establishment. Originally built in the 1700s as a Quaker friends meeting house, the site which houses the Playhouse boasts a fascinating past, and has many myths and legends associated with it. For example, it is believed that there are bodies still buried beneath the existing car park in what was ostensibly unconsecrated ground – a legacy from its Quaker period. In 1849 a 'new' meeting house was built on the same site. Later on, at the turn of the twentieth century, it was owned by the Knights of Saint Columba and named Columba Hall. Subsequently, in 1939, it became a dance hall, and during the Second World War it was used for ammunitions storage. Following the War's end in 1945, Preston Amateur Dramatic Club took the lease on the building and turned it into a theatre, holding their first performance in 1949. Nowadays, several amateur dramatic societies from around the area use this lovely building to stage their productions from September through to June.

Nick Tomlinson, now aged 62 years, has been proudly associated with the Playhouse for over 40 years through his work, both acting and directing here as part of Preston Drama Club. There have been

many tales of hauntings on this site, but it is Nick's story which is the most interesting by far, especially as Nick himself is a staunch sceptic of all things 'spooky'. Nick tells of a true encounter which took place many years ago, when he was in his early twenties and just starting out in drama.

It was a Saturday afternoon, prior to an evening performance, and the theatre was abandoned and quiet, save for Nick who was working in the area of the theatre upstairs which houses the ropes and the lighting. As he quietly went about his business in the dimly lit gallery he heard the sliding door to the gallery slide across and open. Footsteps were then heard walking towards the area he was in. Not expecting anyone to assist him that morning he was both surprised and slightly alarmed, thinking someone had got into the building by some other means than the front entrance, which was locked for security. He could only think that for some reason Alf, who often helped out in the theatre too, had been already in the building when he had first opened up that morning, although as he said later this seemed incredulous. Nick tells me he shouted out to him and at this point fully expected him to reply to his "Alf, Alf, is that you?" As he continued to stare into the shadows of the gallery he distinctly heard the footsteps coming towards him, the sound increasing in volume as they approached closer still. At this point, his hair was on end as he still could see no-one in the gallery. He stood up and walked around and again called out into the other side of the gallery. No reply was forthcoming so he shrugged it off and continued back to where he had been working. Almost at once, he heard the footsteps begin to walk away back towards the door, and again the distinctive sound of the sliding door was heard, then all remained deathly silent.

Not satisfied that this was something 'other-worldly', Nick scoured every inch of the theatre looking for some living soul other than himself. No-one was found within the building and to this day he still recounts the tale with a hint of disbelief. "I am a true sceptic," he said, "and yet I do know that many people have seen or heard things here, including the echoes of an audience clapping. It's just that I am not usually the type; this, however, I would say was inexplicable." One thing he did admit to, though, was the use of an ouija board when he and his young teenage friends were here late at night all those years ago. Is it possible that someone has returned to the Playhouse believing themselves to have been 'invited'?

There is no doubt that some strange events have been reported over the years and Preston Drama group members Margi Shaw and Stella Judson can bear testimony to that. They have been experiencing all kinds of supernatural phenomena here for years. Some of the things that they and others have seen or experienced include the appearance of a dark figure which has been seen in both the dressing rooms in the old cellar *and* in the costume store room upstairs – an area that was once part of the upper balcony. Strange green flashes of light, disgusting odours and sudden icy cold breezes which come and go quickly have also been reported. Another member of the Playhouse cast, at the time a pantomime was being staged, thought she saw someone in costume in this area and, wondering what she was doing in the upper balcony, followed her into the costume area and out through the other side to the lighting gallery, only to find she had quite simply 'disappeared'. It is in this most haunted of areas – the costume store room – that clothes are seen to move along the rails, as if invisible hands could be flicking through the garments searching for their costume. Theatre bookings manager Jane Tudor reports that many of the members of the Playhouse feel uncomfortable at times in the auditorium, and that a 'legless' phantom has been seen by several in the cellar area which now houses the ladies' and gents' toilets. Electrical riggers working here late at night have heard knockings, and again footsteps, just like those first observed 40 years ago by Nick Tomlinson. Not all, but some of these strange paranormal occurrences seem to be attributed to one person, though, and members of the Playhouse now affectionately call him 'Albert' after a team of paranormal researches spent a night investigating the building here and his name came through.

Paranormal researchers began their investigation here one Easter Sunday night last year. Alun Day of Clitheroe Paranormal reported temperature fluctuations from temperate to icy cold, a foul stench and rapid air movements. Flashing green lights were also seen and eventually the group of six made contact with a man who said he was called 'Albert' and who appeared to be looking for his two children, Henry and Margaret, who *he* believed were buried in the unconsecrated ground (now the car park) at the front of the building. Dominic

Wiggan, a local reporter from 'The Valley', accompanied them that night and reported smelling "the most pungent, disgusting, stomach churning stench," which seemed to dissipate as quickly as it arrived.

Jason, myself, and two members of the Preston Drama Club also experienced this phantom stench first hand, on the day we called to take a look around the place ourselves. As we sat talking with our hosts, Alex Tagg, general manager of the Playhouse, and his colleague, a sudden distinctly awful smell wafted in and engulfed us. This was so bad that we had to cover our mouth and nose with our hands. As we talked of possible gas leaks, damp and where the smell might be coming from, it disappeared almost as quickly as it had come. The smell was most pungent and did have an underlying base of sulphur about it, the like of which I have never smelt before.

As we took our leave and thanked our hosts once more, we noticed that the smell had completely gone. Later, as we pondered the overall feel of the Playhouse Theatre, we both decided that we would relish the chance to spend the night in there ourselves – but definitely not alone!

PRESTON TOWN HALL, PRESTON CITY

Something strange is happening down at the Town Hall in Lancaster Road, Preston: lights flickering on and off; strange cold spots in some rooms; doors opening and closing when no-one is there; phantom footsteps heard along empty corridors; and most mysterious of all, a dark spectre floating silently in and out of rooms and up the stairs.

The electrical supply here does seem to be problematic and could perhaps be attributed to paranormal activity. Staff working late at night are all too aware that they must switch off lights as they leave, and yet lights seem to be switched on in the building late at night after all staff have gone home, and staff insist that they turned them off before they left the building. Some who work there report incidents during their working day, where their lights seem to have a life of their own, switching themselves off and then on again. Normal electrical faults have been ruled out as electricians have been called in on many occasions to check the wiring in case of damage. On one occasion, when lights were seen blazing in the Town Hall after hours, the police were called, along with an experienced police dog. After a thorough search of the building, nothing untoward was found. However, rather discon-certingly, nothing would entice the Alsatian into the basement area, despite his handler's best attempts. Staff are flummoxed!

However, it is not just electrical poltergeist activity that is reported. A 'Dickensian' figure has been seen gliding silently along the corridors of power and some cleaning staff refuse to work alone on the strength of it. In fact the cleaners have reported a pleth-ora of ghostly activity when they are in the building after hours, including the sounds of someone moving around in offices that are quite obviously vacant, and doors slamming shut, along with an actual sighting of a mysterious figure in a long coat moving up the staircase.

In 1987, Doug Paterson, who was head porter at the time, saw the ghostly shape of this man, whom many describe as wearing old Victorian style clothing. One night on his shift, long after office hours were over, Doug was walking alone along the dimly lit corridor where this phantom is seen most. As he shined his torch around in the darkness, checking the building was all locked up and safe, he suddenly heard a door open and shut and, suspecting that there may be an intruder in the building, rushed into the room in hot pursuit. He saw the tall figure of a man in a long, dark brown coat – in his words "like a coachman's outfit". Although the 'man' had his back towards him, he could still describe some finer details, even to the extent of the length and colour of his hair, which was grey and quite long over his collar. Doug watched the figure intently, half expecting him to turn around at any moment, at which point he knew would have to confront this stranger and enquire as to how he had got into the building without anyone seeing him, and more importantly, what he was doing there. It must have only been a minute or two that they both stood silently in the darkness just feet away from each other, and by now Doug was beginning to get a sense of something unearthly about this figure, which remained silent and still. As Doug himself stood transfixed, the figure suddenly melted away in front of his very eyes, much to his obvious horror! The episode certainly left Doug with a very creepy feeling for some time afterwards. And Doug also recalls that whilst the figure was in the room a sudden and unexplained cold spot appeared, which caused him to shiver violently and the hairs on the back of his neck to stand up.

These sightings and ghostly phenomena have been reported for at least the last twenty years and continue still to this day. Whilst some staff do have concerns over their night-time visitor, no-one seems too reluctant to get rid of him as he seems relatively harmless. In fact, one staff member, Marjorie Barnes, who was the Mayor's Secretary for over 25 years, when doing an induction for new staff members, incorporated 'their ghost' into the schedule as part of the tour of the Town Hall!

THE HAUNTED SHOE SHOP, PRESTON CITY

Down at a well known shoe Store in Friargate, Preston, something wicked this way comes. Staff there in the 1960s reported odd happenings, most of which led them to believe they were being haunted by a troubled and restless soul (no pun intended!).

For a period of over two years, staff reported incidents as wide ranging as shoe boxes being hurled about, pumps being moved around in their boxes, things jumping off the shelves and light bulbs popping out of their sockets. Not only this, some staff refused to go into the cellar on their own to fetch stock, experiencing a sense of foreboding every time they descended. Shop manageress at the time, Jean Jones, was baffled: "We have weeks go by where nothing happens, then suddenly something 'odd' occurs – now we just say to ourselves, oh no, it's here again!" Jean says she has an open mind about such things, but after so much poltergeist activity she was convinced that this was a serious haunting of some type.

But Jean was not the only one to feel the sharp boot of the phantom pump shifter. Assistant Karen Cooper, aged 17, was reporting for work one morning when she was met with a barrage of flying cardboard shoe boxes coming at her from the shelves in the cellar. She said at the time, "Now I am nervous of going down there into the cellar. I have seen pumps literally turning over in their boxes, I've found burnt paper in the area too. It's all very strange!"

A former local curator of the Harris Museum, Stephen Sartin, had a theory. He believed that the shoe shop may be on the site of an old Catholic chapel which was once located close to the cemetery of the Anglican church of St George's, just behind Friargate. His research showed him that a priest had been buried inadvertently in the Anglican churchyard, which in his opinion may have caused the poor Catholic soul to suffer such unrest at the indignation of it! He did also say, however, that the church dated back to 1734 and hosted many well known people in its graveyard. Another theory offered up was that of a missing grave for one Doctor Richard Shepherd. Despite extensive searches for the gravestone and bodily remains of the doctor, nothing has ever been found, yet records stipulate he was buried here. Mr

Sartin theorised that the events at the shop may well have something to do with this man's terrible fate.

Whatever the reason was for such activity, it held little comfort for the staff who continued to endure the harassment of the flying pumps, boxes and all!

THE GHOST OF NEW HALL LANE, PRESTON CITY

New Hall Lane is just east of the A6 on the A59. This ancient road has its roots in medieval times. With links to the cotton industry, the small rows of terraced houses that backed onto this lane were originally built to house the huge numbers of mill workers who flooded into the area to seek employment during the cotton boom. In the 1820s it became a turnpike road, taking a toll from the scores of travellers who began to traverse this busy thoroughfare. At the western end of the lane, the remarkable Horrocks' Centenary Mill, built in 1891 and which at one time employed over 6,000 people, loomed large on the horizon.

It is in this historic lane that a 'woman in white' is seen and her first recorded sighting was in 1934, when, just days before Christmas, a 29-year-old electrician first saw her ghostly form. Whilst working alone one evening re-wiring an empty shop, he felt a certain unease as dusk approached. He was in an upstairs room when the feelings turned to something much more concrete as a terrifying figure appeared before him in what he described as a "long white shroud, which shimmered like satin". As he stared in abject terror at the shape that had manifested itself before him, his skin began to crawl, as the hairs upon his neck and arms stood upright and his scalp tingled with fear. He described her as almost "rising from beneath the floorboards" in a misty form, then seeming to become more solid. As she took on a more human form he could see her eyes, dark and brooding, almost black in colour, glaring back at him, and her long, dark straggly hair hung down to her shoulders. At that point, unable to contain his terror any longer, he dropped his tools and ran headlong down the stairs, two at a time!

As news of this strange phantom appearance in the shop spread, the owner of the shop, finding the story quite incredulous, arranged to let four hardy men stay in the premises all night to see if anything of a paranormal nature happened to them. Along with this motley crew, a *Lancashire Evening Post* reporter was in attendance to verify, or not, any incidents, spooky or otherwise. Two of the men were highly excited about the prospect and claimed an interest in all things ghostly, one of them seeming to have some psychic ability, as on the night he 'saw' a woman in the room with them at some point and claimed her name was Margaret and that she did indeed have black hair and dark eyes. The other man also saw what he described as a strange white mist hovering in the exact same area as the alleged sighting of 'Margaret'.

To perhaps solve the mystery of the phantom lady with staring eyes we can look to the past inhabitants. According to a previous tenant of the shop, Mr Harry Seed of Preston, whose family once owned the shop, locals remember a dreadful tragedy that took place there around 1907. At that time a local butcher occupied the premises. It is believed that the butcher murdered his wife because of her drinking habits and subsequent infidelity. It was Mr Seed's father who later bought the shop, but he never lived in it because of its macabre history. Could this be the lady who haunts this shop, is she seeking justice or revenge for her untimely murder? Locals still believe that the tragic events that unfolded at that time in this unassuming shop have led to the haunting of the 'phantom with the staring eyes'.

CABARET FANCY DRESS, ASHTON-UPON-RIBBLE

Built for workers constructing the railway in the late Victorian era, the terraced houses on Tulketh Brow end with a corner shop now run as a fancy dress agency called Cabaret Fancy Dress.

Business manager Maggie Murray told me that the shop is home to at least one ghost who causes trouble by moving costumes and props around when they have been sorted ready for collection. In recent years a fur cat costume had been made to order for a customer and was hanging in a sealed bag ready for fitting, but when the customer arrived the 'head' was not in the bag. A thorough search failed to find it and Maggie made another to replace it. Weeks later it was found in the cleaning cupboard under the sink.

One of Maggie's staff members, Maureen, sadly lost her mother's diamond wedding ring in the shop one day. She was particularly upset as her mother had recently passed away and the ring was very special to her. Amidst the clutter of costumes finding it again seemed unlikely, but several days later it appeared in the middle of the floor – on the date of her mother's 60th wedding anniversary!

The identity of the ghost haunting the shop in a mystery, but Maggie is convinced that it is 'Elvis' telling her that he is unhappy she is making money hiring out Elvis suits!

DB MEX RESTAURANT, PRESTON CITY

In June 2005, whilst conducting research for this book, I was contacted by the owner of an underground Mexican restaurant in Preston city. Standing on one of the oldest roads in the city, DB Mex is owned by Knicki Jones, who told me that her staff have reported unexplainable events and cold spots for some years and that a local psychic who often comes in for lunch had stated that the building might be haunted. I decided to go along and see for myself and, accompanied by Veronica, enjoyed a delicious meal before setting off on a full investigation of the building.

Local records show that the building was the site of the first reading and lecture rooms of he Preston Institution for the Diffusion of Knowledge, which is now the University of Central Lancashire. The institution was set up to allow poorer people to have access to books. A plaque owned by Knicki commemorates this historical fact, but the building has yet another claim to fame: it was the original birthplace of the Temperance Movement, which was formed by Joseph Livesey and seven other men in 1832 when they signed a declaration never to drink alcohol again. In more recent years the building was used as a nightclub called Cheeky Monkeys before coming under Knicki's management in 1996.

Knicki explained that various parts of the building were in a state of renovation, which is why the current restaurant area is accessed by a staircase and is essentially underground. In the past people have reported a variety of phenomena, including noises coming from a storage area, such as a very loud thumping noise for which no explanation can be found, as well as shadowy figures and spectral touches on the skin, and even a female figure which was sighted over the 2004 Christmas period.

We decided to visit the room above the current restaurant, which is used for storing building materials and is not usually open to the public. As soon as we entered Veronica sensed that there was a man present: "There is a man here, strutting around like a peacock." She likened his appearance to Abraham Lincoln and described him as being in control of proceedings which were going on around him; he had thin hair and a long handlebar moustache and was wearing a tailored frock coat with an expensive looking gold pocket watch on a chain. "He says he is surprised to see us tonight," said Veronica. "He is showing me his little finger, which looks deformed or severed, his name is Joseph." Could this have been the spirit of Joseph Livesey perhaps? "There are books here too, books everywhere," proclaimed Veronica. Knicki confirmed that this room had been the library of the Institute for the Diffusion of Knowledge. "There are street beggars as well, many of them, and women draped in shawls." This was also correct as the purpose of the Institution was to allow poorer folk access to literature.

After the sudden psychic wave which hit Veronica as we entered the area, the spirits seemed to depart as quickly as they had arrived and there was no further information to be gleaned. We took some photographs as we left in case anything was still around and later discovered that on one shot of the staircase next to the old library a strange misty form appeared which we are still unable to explain. Could this be the ghost of Joseph Livesey making his final stand against Knicki for selling alcoholic spirits on the premises where centuries earlier he had decried alcohol forever?

Despite the number of spirits sensed by Veronica, none of them seemed malevolent, merely psychic echoes of the past which still leave a chill(i) in the air!

CHAPTER FIVE

GRAVE SECRETS

THE DEVIL HOUSE, PRESTON CITY

Some places are haunted by the lost and troubled souls of men, women, children, and yes, sometimes animals. But in one street in Preston the Devil himself allegedly resides!

Way back in the annals of time – 1837 to 1840 to be exact – Preston was the headquarters for the Church of Jesus Christ of Latter-day Saints, widely known as the LDS Church or the Mormon Church. And although a small time capsule in history, most of the first British Mormons emigrated to America from this very area. Today, Preston is still the oldest continuous branch of the Mormon Church in the world. It was in this house of modest proportions on Fox Street that Elder Hebert C. Kimball, Elder Orson Hyde, Elder William Richards and three others wrestled with the forces of darkness and their principle, old Beelzebub, Lucifer, Prince of the Underworld, or as we might know him best, the Devil.

The elders arrived in Preston on the 22nd July 1837 intending to stay in these rooms for the first two weeks in order to carry out their important work in Preston. However, following the dramatic events in the early hours of the 30th July, they moved out again immediately, after the very first baptism to take place, that of Sister Ann Dawson who resided at 21 Pole Street.

On that night, it is said, the Devil seemed to take it upon himself to attack the Elders in an attempt to stop their work, unleashing a host of demons and evil spirits from Hell. Elder Isaac Russell was attacked first, and as the evil forces possessed him he appealed to Elder Kimball to cast them out. As Elders Kimball and Hyde gave Elder Russell a priesthood blessing (or exorcism) in the upstairs room, Elder Kimball also fell foul of 'Old Nick' and was viciously attacked by the forces of evil, eventually rendering him unconscious. His written statement of what followed is a powerful account of the lengths to which they claimed the Devil went in order to stop these god-fearing and devout religious men. According to Elder Kimball, writing his account later:

"The first thing I recollected was being supported by Elders Hyde and Richards, who were praying for me, Elder Richards having followed Russell up to my room. Elders Hyde and Richards then assisted me to get on the bed, but my agony was so great I could not endure it, and I arose, bowed my knees and prayed. I then arose and sat upon the bed, when a vision was opened to our minds, and we could distinctly see the evil spirits, who foamed and gnashed their teeth at us. We gazed upon them about an hour and a half (by Willard's watch). We were not looking towards the window, but towards the wall. Space appeared before us, and we saw the devils coming in legions, with their leaders, who came within a few feet of us.

They came towards us like armies rushing to battle. They appeared to be men of full stature, possessing every form and feature of men in the flesh, who were angry and desperate; and I shall never forget the vindictive malignity depicted on their countenances as they looked me in the eye. Any attempt to paint the scene which then presented itself, or portray their malice and enmity, would be vain. We distinctly heard those spirits talk and express their wrath and hellish designs against us. However, the Lord delivered us from them, and blessed us exceedingly that day."

Through the power of good triumphing over evil, the Elders were spared and Elder Kimball recovered that fateful morning sufficiently to conduct the baptismal service of Ann Dawson as planned. Later that morning over 9,000 people watched the baptisms take place in the River Ribble. Subsequently, however, obviously still troubled by his diabolic encounter, Elder Kimball began to have doubts over his faith and his ability to be fruitful and productive in the Mormon Church, fearing that it was his unworthiness that had somehow brought the attack upon them. It was not until later that he found faith in himself again, when he discussed his new found fears over his faith and his worthiness to complete God's work, and realised the extent and power of the evil forces which had raged within him, albeit only temporarily. On his return to the United States, he greatly agonised over the event with the prophet Joseph Smith and subsequently realised the real reason for the attack. In response to the question about his personal worthiness, the prophet replied:

"No, Brother Heber, at that time you were nigh unto the Lord; there was only a veil between you and him, but you could not see him. When I heard of it, it gave me great joy, for I knew that the work of God had taken root in that land. It was this that caused the devil to make a struggle to kill you. The nearer a person approaches the Lord, a greater power will be manifested by the adversary to prevent the accomplishment of his purposes." (Quote taken from a text from the late 1800s.)

In recent times, Wilfred Street lodgings has seen many incarnations as a home and later as business offices. A solicitor's office was housed within these historic walls for nearly thirty years but rather disconcertingly the property has been on the market for sale for over six years now and still has no buyer ... I wonder why?

The Warren, Leyland

This large Edwardian house behind the council offices in Leyland was built by a businessman for his managing director in 1905. It is now a funeral home and my informant, who wishes to remain anonymous, told me of the strange 'Toast Ghost' she lived with during her nine-year incumbency:

"My husband is a funeral director and when we decided to move north from London the house seemed perfect. But I had no idea we were adopting a ghost when we moved in! It all began late one night when I woke up to the strong smell of toast cooking. I assumed it was the children but when I went downstairs there was no-one around. It happened several times after that incident, and then I began to hear footsteps following me around as I was tidying up. I asked one of the cleaners if the house was haunted and at first she told me it wasn't – probably wanting me to settle in – but she later admitted there was a ghost, and that it manifested itself as the scent of toast cooking! Another time, approximately a year afterwards, the same cleaner remarked 'you must be having something nice for lunch' as she passed me in the hall one day. I replied that I hadn't planned anything special and we both went into the kitchen to find the strong smell of fresh toast again, but on this occasion we both smelled it. We lived happily in that house between 1996 and 2005 and I have fond memories of the 'Toast Ghost' – it became part of our family really."

St Mary's Church, Bamber Bridge

One of the strangest forms of ghostly experience is that which is commonly termed 'timeslip'. They are a rare type of encounter, and as such are a gem to be unearthed by the serious psychic researcher. This story concerns a timeslip encounter described to me by an informer I shall call Bill, who reported the experience to me and his colleague, Valerie.

Bill and Valerie had been great friends for years and had spent many afternoons visiting sites around their home town of Bamber Bridge, so it wasn't the first time they had decided to take a walk up to St Mary's Church on that golden summer's day in June 2000.

"The day somehow felt strange," Bill described, "it was almost unreal, the colours of the trees, the sunlight and the entire ambience of the place seemed strangely different in a way I can't easily describe in words. I mentioned this to Valerie and she also felt peculiar." This is one of the commonly reported features in timeslip encounters, where the percipients feel somewhat disconnected with the world around them, as if they are temporarily experiencing life from a different angle. Bill continued, telling me that they walked around the churchyard, which was quiet and deserted, and then went inside the church, stopping to look at the architecture before heading out of the main door at the front of the church.

"As we went out the door a group of between ten and fifteen people walked in and bustled silently past us; they went into a doorway on the right hand side which had a sign on it saying 'Bell Ringers Only' and ascended a spiral staircase. I recall at the time feeling weird as they passed by in silence and dressed in clothes akin to 1970s styles. A couple of minutes later, after pondering their strange appearance, I asked Valerie what she had thought of them, and she agreed they had seemed out of the ordinary and that the whole time they had been in the church and churchyard somehow hadn't felt quite right. We turned around and went back, determined to see them again and put our minds at rest."

But when they arrived back at the church they were met with a sight they had not expected to see. The doorway that the group of people had passed through was still there, but when they opened it they found a brick wall covered in dust and cobwebs; clearly it had been like that for some time. When they examined the exterior wall of that section of the church there was no evidence of the staircase they had seen either. Confused and dazed by what had happened, and at a loss to offer each other any valid explanation, they left the church and returned home.

It wasn't until several years later that they spoke of the strange experience they had shared and decided to re-visit the church to try to find a logical explanation. Unfortunately the whole area had been

refurbished when they returned and there was no sign of the bricked up doorway, the staircase or the sign.

In an attempt to offer an explanation for their experience I visited the church in question with Ian in September 2005. It was a bright autumn day and the sunlight streamed through the trees, just as it had done on that day in June 2000, but there was no evidence of a former doorway, no silent bell ringers and no staircase to be seen. One thought did occur to me whilst walking among the lichen-covered gravestones, though: what if they had decided to follow the group up the staircase? Where would they have ended up? What would have happened to them? Would they have crossed over into a parallel world? Perhaps the answer is best left unknown …

The Vicarage, Croston, Leyland

An old work colleague of mine told me this curious tale about a haunting at Croston vicarage where a close friend of his used to live. Apparently it is common knowledge in the local area that the house is haunted by the spirit of a little girl.

After living for many years in the vicarage the family had only experienced mild supernatural phenomena, including unexplained sounds and movements of objects, but that all changed early one morning when the mother of the family was coming out of the garage at the side of the house. As she turned the corner of the house she saw a young girl walking alone across the road. She waved and called 'hello', at which point the child looked straight at her and waved merrily back. She thought no more of it until later that day when it occurred to her that it was very early for a child that young to be walking around alone on a public highway. Minutes later a neighbour who had lived in the area all her life knocked on the door and she asked the neighbour if she had also seen the girl. Unsurprisingly, she had not, and it was only then that the mother described in detail the appearance of the child, which, she was informed by the neighbour, matched exactly that of the spirit child reputed to haunt the vicarage.

Eastview, Deepdale, Preston

The ancient Pagan winter solstice 'Yule' takes place on the 21st–22nd December each year. It is a time when energies of a spiritual nature are said to be stronger and the likelihood of experiencing something other worldly in increased.

It was on this day in 1999 that two friends of mine were walking past the church of St Ignatius when suddenly one of their daughters, aged three at the time, declared, "there's a ghost in that tree mummy," and indicated a large tree on the opposite side of the road. Mummy – Carry – replied "really, who is it?" Her daughter replied that it was 'a man' and as they continued walking she looked back at the tree, smiled and waved.

Strangely this encounter was not the only time the same child seemed to 'see' something that those around her could not. On moving into a new Victorian terraced property on Eastview built in 1856, the same daughter told her mother that there was a 'man ghost' which she had seen both in the hallway and on the staircase. Weeks later Carry herself experienced a bizarre sensation in the cellar of the house and made a swift exit up the stairs. On another occasion a bicycle which had been propped up against a wall in the back room of the house was found on its side with one pedal completely unscrewed from the frame and lying discarded over the other side of the room!

As far as I am aware the haunting seemed to calm down as the family settled into their new home and they lived very happily there for several years. It is interesting to note that the young daughter witnessed the full apparitions, not only in the house but also apparently in a tree at St Ignatius church nearby. It is so often the case that children under the age of ten are more susceptible to the sensitive vibrations of the spirit world – perhaps because they are not yet conditioned to believe that such things do not exist.

CHAPTER SIX

A GAGGLE OF GHOSTS

MILEY & TULKETH VIADUCT, PRESTON CITY

Train tracks are always dangerous, but Miley Tunnel in Preston may be more dangerous than most, as it is believed to be haunted by many of the tragic souls who have lost their lives here.

From as long ago as the Victorian period, dark and beckoning tunnels have drawn people to them and many have lost their lives because of this strange, magnetic pull. On a fateful December in 1866, a group of young girls gathered around to see a train come in to Deepdale Station – once a frequent haunt of many an avid train spotter, as the steam locomotives of the day were considered quite a novelty in these days. No one knows for sure what prompted passenger Harry Whittaker to extend his arm to one of the girls as she moved forward towards the edge of the platform, just as the train was moving off. But sadly she did take his hand and despite the shouts of the terrified onlookers she refused to let go and twisted and fell beneath the wheel of the train to her instant death. Such horror has been replayed over and over in the tunnels since then, as many have reported hearing her agonising screams, and some rather foolish souls, who venture into the tunnels in games of dare, see her shadowy form in the tunnel still. Many other children during the early history of the steam train met their death here as the fascination with this new mode of transport drew them into the tunnel to play hide and seek. Local residents in Burrows Road in Deepdale often report hideous shrieks of pain and terror as the ghosts of these unfortunates re-live their last minutes of agonising death.

Other stretches of this now infamous track are also home to the departed. Built in 1840, the Tulketh Brow viaduct was considered a major engineering feat of its day. However, the men and boys who worked on this engineering masterpiece were all too aware of the dangers of building the tunnels and dreaded every one in its construction. When it came to the fateful ninth arch, fourteen men and two boys were crushed as the incomplete framework of the archway crashed down on top of them, their screams resonating through the countryside sending a chill through many a living soul. Luckily, most escaped with broken bones and bloodied and bruised limbs, but one man – Edward Lewis – whilst being pulled from the rubble, died from his terrible injuries right there in the ninth archway. Three others also lost their lives within the next few days, their injuries being too severe to survive. All four men are said to haunt this viaduct, their dreadful deaths recorded psychically in the very fabric of the bricks and mortar that remain.

Today, sadly, thrill seekers still play dare here and only recently in 2003 an article in the *Lancashire Evening Post* stated that police declared Preston's Miley Tunnel a potential death trap following an accident that killed a Fulwood student who fell 40 ft beside the disused line on Christmas Day. What is it that draws sane, logical people to this stretch of tunnel – is it the desperate soul of the first young girl who died in 1866, or is there something else which lurks there, waiting to take the souls of the unsuspecting? Please don't try to find out!

AVENHAM PARK, PRESTON CITY

A curious tale found its way into my archives some years ago concerning a phantom Roman legion near Avenham Park. My correspondent's mother recalled the story from her childhood years around 1940:

"I was playing in a field near to where we used to live, opposite Avenham Park. As I looked across the river I could see a lot of men, marching towards the city. It was strange because I remember thinking they must be very short as they appeared only a few feet tall, but then I realised they were walking 'in the ground', as if on a different level of land. The next day I told my teacher at school what I had seen and she showed me some pictures in a book which corresponded to the appearance of the soldiers I had watched a day earlier."

Interestingly, the city has strong Roman connections and it is known that they came to Preston during the Roman invasion of Britain. Watling Street Road – which keeps its name to this day – is part of an ancient Roman road which ran from Preston (or Priest Town in those times) in the direction of Goosnargh and Chingle Hall, where traces of former Roman habitation have been uncovered, and indications also of a possible Roman villa.

THE BANNISTER DOLL, PRESTON

Most Prestonians will either know, or have someone in their family who has heard of, the chilling ghost story of Bannister Doll. Sightings of the Bannister Doll – the name given to the ghost of a young Victorian girl who was flogged to death publicly by her own father – have been reported by many past generations of Preston residents and it is believed that her spirit still continues to haunt to this day.

Approximately 150 years ago, the eminent Mr Bannister, who local legend tells us was believed to be a mayor or a wealthy mill owner, lived in his large house at the top of Snow Hill, which is off Walker Street in Preston. When his unmarried daughter, Dorothy, came to him and confessed that she was with child (a damning and shameful admission by the standards of the day), so enraged was he that he dragged her by her hair out into the street, tied her to a nearby stake and whipped her until her blood ran in the streets. Naturally, she did not survive the beating. The story goes that later the father learned that his young daughter had in fact been raped and he realised to his horror that he had murdered a poor little innocent. She later became known as Bannister Doll, some say due to her doll-like appearance because her face was 'painted' with pale make-up, like a china doll, such was the fashion of the day. Some said that her name was Dolly Bannister and that this was where her nickname originated, but others attributed her name to the fact that when she was seen in spectral form she took on the shade of a ghostly white.

It is often believed that at the scene of horrific murders such as this a psychic imprint can be left upon the area. This psychic imprint can be likened to a video recording, almost as if those first shocking events are doomed to be continually played out time and time again. This, then, may possibly explain why her frail and sometimes bloodied form is reputed to haunt the streets around this area and also in the vicinity of the Holy Trinity Church, where her battered body was finally laid to rest.

Mr Bill Procter reported in the *Lancashire Evening Post* in 1984 that he himself spent time in the very same house where Bannister Doll once lived. He was only a young child, but he still remembers what an eerie old place it was. Although he does not recall seeing anything himself, his father must have been so unnerved by some aspect of the building that he and the family only managed to spend three days in the old Bannister home, promptly moving out after this time to another area. Other families who lived here tell tales of shrieks in the night, the sound of heavy footsteps and the slamming of doors in anger. As the stories spread, so did the Doll's reputation for vengeance. It was believed that any mysterious deaths, particularly of young men, were attributable to her wrath.

Young and old alike feared Bannister Doll and the legend took many forms. Not only was her name and its origins in dispute, so too was the way in which she died and where. Local folklore speaks of her being tethered to a huge stone slab at the corner of Ladywell Street and Heatley Street – in fact, such a stone bearing the date 1850 was found in this area where these two streets joined on what is now British Rail land. Others tell of her being chained to the banisters of her home before being flogged to death in the house. Some believe that she was flogged in the street outside her home. Wherever her actual demise took place, her reign of terror covers many areas, as some have even reported seeing her in the area where Bannister Hall (now demolished) stood in Higher Walton; a mysterious 'White Lady' haunts this particular area too – is she one and the same?

Stephen Sartin in *The People and Places of Historic Preston* (Carnegie Press, 1988), notes that no mayor or prominent mill owner is recorded as living in this area at this time. However, he does point out that a John Bannister was governor of the house of correction which was located on the site of the now demolished friary, where the A59 bypass is currently. There was, apparently, a Dorothy amongst his family names, and indeed some of the mayors of Preston had been from the Bannister line. Could this be our Bannister Doll?

In the 1980s, particularly, this local ghost story reached fever pitch as several newspaper reporters began to receive numerous reports of her haunting these areas once more. Many came forward to tell of the feelings of terror they experienced whilst having to frequent these streets, sometimes late at night. Her ghost is said to take on many forms and to petrify those who come near her 'home ground'. A glowing bright light, eerie footsteps, a small child, a young woman in a white bonnet, and even a black dog, have been attributed to Bannister Doll's residual energy. Whatever her form, it is no wonder she seeks retribution if she was, as is believed, murdered by her own father for no other reason than of being the unfortunate victim of a terrible crime.

BIBLIOGRAPHY

Publications:
Jason Karl's Great Ghost Hunt by Jason Karl, New Holland, 2004
An Illustrated History of the Haunted World by Jason Karl, New Holland, 2007
21st Century Ghosts by Jason Karl, New Holland, 2007
Haunted Places of Lancashire by Jason Karl, Countryside Books, 2006
Ghosts of North West England by Peter Underwood, Fontana, 1978.
The Ghosts of Lancashire by Muriel Armand, Print Origination, 1993.
Haunted Sites of Oldham by Janette Quinlan and Shaun McGrath, Oldham Education and Leisure, 1999.
Supernatural Lancashire by Peter Hough, Hale, 2003.
Ghosts of the North by Melanie Warren and Tony Wells, Broadcast Books, 1995.
Lancashire's Ghosts and Legends by Terence Whitaker, Granada, 1982.
Ghosts, Traditions and Legends of Old Lancashire by Ken Howarth, Sigma Leisure, 1993.
North Country Ghosts and Legends by Terence Whitaker, Grafton Books, 1988.
Lancashire Ghosts by Kathleen Eyre, Dalesman, 1989.
Haunted Halls of Lancashire by Keith Hassall and Mike Firth, Lancashire Books, 1990.
From a Saint to a King by Alec Price, Moorland Publishing, 2005.
The Story of Alston Hall by Marian Roberts, Alston Hall Residential College, 1994.
The Alston Hall Trail by Graham Wilkinson, Alston Hall Residential College, 2000.
The People and Places of Historic Preston by Stephen Sartin, Carnegie Press, 1988.

Periodicals:

Lancashire Life article by Caroline Renshaw, October 1994.
Lancashire Evening Post, various.
Preston Citizen, various.
Leyland Today, June 2006.

Television:

Ghost Hunters, Inca Productions, 1997.

ADDRESSES

The Wheatsheaf Inn
34 Woodplumpton Road, Woodplumpton, Preston PR4 0NE.
01772 690301

The Railway Inn.
115 Station Road, Kirkham, Preston, Lancashire PR4 2HD.
01772 687753

The Old Hob Inn
Bamber Bridge, Preston, Lancashire PR5 6EP.
01772 33686

Alston Hall
Alston Lane, Longridge, Preston, Lancashire PR3 3BP.
01772 784661
www.alstonhall.com

Samlesbury Hall
Preston New Road, Samlesbury, Preston, Lancashire PR5 0UP.
01254 812010
www.samlesburyhall.co.uk

Hoghton Tower
Hoghton, Preston, Lancashire PR5 0SH.
01254 852986
www.hoghtontower.co.uk

Park Hall
Charnock Richard, Chorley, Lancashire PR7 5LP.
www.parkhall-hotel.co.uk

Haighton Manor
Haighton Green Lane, Haighton, Preston PR2 5SQ.
01772 663170
www.haightonmanor.net

Cabaret Fancy Dress
44 Tulketh Brow, Preston, Lancashire PR2 2SD.
01772 723773

DB Mex. 21 Cannon Street, Preston PR1 3NR.
01772 558600
Open Tuesday–Saturday